FARMWIVES in PROFILE

17 Women:
17 candid questions
about their lives

Photos & Recipes

BILLI J MILLER
writer & photographer

FriesenPress

Suite 300 - 990 Fort St
Victoria, BC, Canada, V8V 3K2
www.friesenpress.com

Copyright © 2015 by Billi J Miller
First Edition — 2015

All photographs taken by, provided by, and copyright of Billi J Miller with the exception of Lois Purser which was "provided".

Answers to all the "interview questions" provided by: the "farmwives" and used by their permission.

Answers for the section: "What is the impact your Mother has had on your lives?" section provided by: families of the "Farmwives".

Cover design by FriesenPress
Book design and production by FriesenPress
Author photograph by Billi-Jean Miller.

ISBN
978-1-4602-7763-8 (Paperback)
978-1-4602-7764-5 (eBook)

1. Biography & Autobiography

Distributed to the trade by The Ingram Book Company

Contents

To Dean, Madeline and Kate: for showing me "home".

To Rebecca K: your community will hold you and your daughters forever in our hearts. Donald will never be forgotten. You are truly a farmwife like no other.

"The house does not rest on the ground, but upon a woman."
Mexican proverb

PREFACE:

Until 2009, I had been a career-minded 30-something woman living on my own in Edmonton, Alberta, Canada. Everything changed in August of that year when I met my husband to be. Around a year later, when the relationship developed, I found myself living two and a half hours east of Edmonton on a nearly 100-year old farm. The setting was starkly different. Primarily agricultural, many of the families who lived here had been here for a century or more. The rich heritage was traditional, but yet mixed with "newer" and bustling sectors of energy and a booming oil industry. I was charmed by the dichotomy and how steeped and proud the tradition was that remained here. Decades-old quaint community halls dotted the landscape. Occasionally, we'll still see these same halls filled by neighbors celebrating milestones, or getting together for an evening card game. Rustic and beautiful remnants of one-room schoolhouses remained – telling silent stories of generations past.

While I am far from a historian – I can provide a basic history of "my new home" through the people that live here. Many European settlers came here in the beginning of the 1900's as a result of the Canadian Governments' effort to populate and develop the Prairies. After successful marketing and a promise of "bountiful" harvests and an "invigorating" winter, many Europeans came to this area (as well as, to the rest of the Prairies) to develop a 160-acre parcel for a ten-dollar fee.[1] Their job; to break the land, and create a homestead.

1   http://www.historymuseum.ca/cmc/exhibitions/cmc/acres/acrese.shtml

Many of those that live here, proudly speak of how their family farm was settled in the first and second decades of the 20th century. I now live on one of those farms and am married to a fourth-generation farmer.

While the stories of these (mostly male) settlers are hearty and dramatic – my aim of this book is to bring focus and light to the generations of women whose stories are sometimes left out of history books. Although, many "new" farm families are seeing changes to the roles of women, this book focuses on celebrating the "traditional" farmwife.

I have spent two and a half years interviewing seventeen women between the ages of fifty-five and ninety about their lives as farm-wives. Their interview answers are minimally edited, and essentially verbatim. This preserves the authenticity of the women and their stories.

My deepest thanks goes out to these seventeen women for sitting down and sharing their hearts with me. In doing so, they have shown me what strength, gratitude and beauty truly look like. Their love for their husbands and children shine through in who they are. Their presence in their families and in their communities is irreplaceable beyond words. They all have unique and differing stories. All of which, result in a beautiful portrayal of rural life in the Prairies of Western Canada. I hope you enjoy it.

INTRODUCTION:

When I relocated in 2010 to the country from the big city to marry the "Farmer of my dreams" - I was very quickly taken aback by the amazing contributions of farmwives. Without them, the true meaning of "community" would be impossible. From baking for events at community halls, to hosting "showers" welcoming new community members. To delivering warm meals to hungry farmers harvesting the fields, to the limitless other tasks for their farms and their families – these women have been the foundation.

These women have been pillars - not only in their homes and in their families – but also in their communities. This book celebrates them, their life's work, and their passionate dedication to the larger patchwork of Canada's Heritage.

I believe there is no such thing as an "unremarkable" Mother. When I approached each of these women to be a part of this project, their humility and unassuming natures shone. "I haven't done anything special, I'm just a farmwife", or "I've just done what all the others before me had done" was a common reply.

The collection of women I have interviewed is, by no means, exhaustive. I interviewed only a mere sampling of these women in my community and nearby. There are countless more of them scattered throughout the Prairies of Western Canada and beyond. Their remarkable dedication and devotedness to their families and communities is nothing short of amazing. My purpose for completing this project has been to shed light on their tireless devotion and to hold them up to their communities, to give them the recognition they deserve and to truly honor them.

This book details: seventeen heartfelt questions and answers about each woman's life as a farmwife, beautiful photos, and of course, recipes!

As an added surprise to some of the "farmwives" – many the families submitted a statement at the end of their interviews on the "impact their Mom has had on their life". It's a touching tribute that is not to be missed.

My deep wish for this book - is for it to serve as an intimate and culinary portrayal of this geographic area, and the amazing women in it. I also hope it fills the farmwives with honor and pride for the beautiful lives they have lived.

FARMWIFE INTERVIEW #1
Name: Edith Paul

Edith and Albert Paul proudly show off the letter they
received from Buckingham Palace in honor of their 65th
wedding anniversary. Albert sadly passed away in April 2015,
during the writing of this book. Age at this writing: 84

1. How long have you lived in this community?
   I have lived in my community of Thomasville all of my life.

2. What was your background prior to marrying your husband?
   I worked on the farm.

3. How long have you been married, and if you have children - how many do you have?
   (Points to her sign above the kitchen "Paul Family - Est. 1949"). I married Albert at 19 years in 1949. We have six children.

4. What has the role of farmwife meant to you?
   Long days and hard work. Milking cows, feeding pigs, shoveling grain.

5. What has your husbands' role been?
   All the outside farm work, but worked together. We farmed approximately a half section, but we fenced for the County too.

6. What is the best part, for you, in this life as a farmwife?
   The teamwork.., because, we kept our family together as a family.

7. What is the hardest part?
   The financial stress.

8. Was feeling isolated ever a part of living on the farm? If so, how did you deal with it?
   Maybe in the beginning, because we were back in the bush. Roads weren't established yet. We shoveled miles and miles to get out of storms.

9. Were there any "new" traditions that you started in your family? (and may have passed down to your children)?
   I passed down cooking, canning and baking. I tried to get the kids to clean the inside of chickens, but they wouldn't!

10. Was there anything you were not prepared for, prior to becoming a farmwife?

> There was a lot more to it than I thought … … a lot more responsibility.

11. Were there any expectations of you that proved especially difficult for you?

> Stooking crops, thrashing.

12. Was there anything that you would have liked to (or that you did) change?

> Yes … A LOT of diapers!!!!

13. If there was a legacy that you'd like to leave behind from your life here, what would you like it to be? (Such as: your proudest accomplishment, or something important that you instilled in your children)?

> Just be yourself … help out. I was famous for my donuts.

14. What is your fallback recipe when you're too tired to plan for supper?

> Pancakes.

15. We've all had unexpected guests pop in. What was a trick that you used to ensure you were always prepared for company?

> Canned food … we used food we had on the farm.

16. Do you have any words of advice for women who may be marrying a farmer today?

> Learn a lot about the life you're getting into.

17. What is a key piece of advice you could give to keep a marriage strong?

> You have to work together and try to agree on what goes on. Be realistic … compromise. You're going to disagree because everyone has an opinion.

RECIPE FROM EDITH PAUL:
BUNS:

Ingredients:

2 eggs beaten
6 tbsp oil
½ cup sugar
½ tsp salt
3 cups warm water
2 tsp yeast or 1 pkg
7-9 cups flour

Directions: Mix oil, sugar, salt, water, and eggs together. Add 2 cups flour, stir and, add yeast. Add remaining flour. Oil bowl, put mixture in to rise. Punch every 15 mins for 1 hour. Make into buns, rise for 1 hour. Put in oven at 400C – should get 3 dozen buns.

WHAT IS THE IMPACT YOUR MOTHER HAS HAD ON YOUR LIVES?

"When the children of Edith Paul sat down together to reminisce about what our Mother means to us we were all somewhat overwhelmed by what she has gone through in her life and how many of her traits have been passed on to the generations that follow her. We thought back to our youth on the farm and the tremendous amount of work our mother did. At the time we all thought it was just normal that mom did the majority of the household chores, without the luxury of running water, then went out and helped with daily farm duties like milking the cows twice a day, helping with the pigs as well as everything needed with the chickens. She always had a huge garden that many of the children reluctantly helped with but we were all quick to reap the rewards of. She also worked side by side with her husband every day, making fence posts, fencing, stooking, seeding, harvesting and hundreds of other jobs too numerous to mention.

Our mother is an excellent cook. We can all remember the fresh baked bread, stealing a little for fried dough, fried chicken Sunday's and of course mom's wonderful donuts.

Mom was and remains very community minded, always helping anyone regardless the cause.

Our Mom is a rare and wonderful woman. She is everything that a mother should be and more. We truly love her for the strength she offers us, the comfort she continuously show us, the support she provides us and the magnitude of love that she unselfishly shares. She is an amazing and precious mother, grandmother, great grandmother and friend. "

By, the children of Edith Paul

FARMWIFE INTERVIEW #2
Name: Emily Welsh

Age at this writing: 89

- -

** Author's note: you'll note that some of the questions in this particular interview were left blank. If you have ever made the acquaintance of this woman, you
would understand why. The particular answers left out, were those that could
have had some negative component to them. The wonder of this charming lady
is that few people near her have ever heard her be negative.

Farmwives in Profile

1. How long have you lived in this community?

   The Knor Family emigrated from Nebraska, USA. Joe Knor came in 1929, built a house on the section he bought at Paradise Valley. March, 1930 Joe and Julia Knor sans Emil and Frank, daughter Emma (Emily) came to their new home. I lived at this farm until 2000 when my husband, Bert Welsh and I moved to our new home at Horizon Village Parkview, Lloydminster, Alberta.

2. What was your background prior to marrying your husband?

   I went to Paradise Valley School for Grades 1-9. Then to Camrose Lutheran College for my High School Graduating June 1944. I attending Edmonton Normal School which was at the Garneau School. I taught at Botha, Golden Valley, Wildwood and Paradise Valley, retired in 1961.

3. How long have you been married, and if you have children - how many do you have?

   Bert Welsh and I were married August 17, 1949. We bought my folks farm 1950 and went farming. We celebrated our 51st Anniversary in 2000. We had two sons Marvin and Glenn. Bert passed away January 2001. I have five special grandchildren.

4. What has the role of farmwife meant to you?

   Farming was a wonderful life. Bert and I worked together. We had cattle, pigs, chickens, pet dog, and cats (outside). Bert had his saddle horse for a few years. Loved harvest time. Bert combined and I drove the grain truck. When the boys grew up, they were a great help. I loved my garden, little orchard, flowers, and mowing the lawn. The farm was our happy family life. Wonderful memories.

5. What has your husbands' role been?

   Bert liked his animals, especially cattle. Had registered pigs. Bert was a mechanic in the world war so he worked on vehicles and machinery. He worked on the municipal county roads driving caterpillar equipment before. He was a great, organized farmer. When our family came he was a happy Dad, loved playing with them, then with hockey and ball. It was great when they helped him do farm work.

6. What is the best part, for you, in this life as a farmwife?

It was a family working together. The great country space - spring new growth, walks in the pasture and fields, the animals, wildlife. The boys loved to ride their bikes, motor-bikes, snare and shoot gophers, magpies and crows. They learned to drive vehicles and tractors. Loved having their friends at the farm to play with. Birthdays were special.

7. What is the hardest part?

I would say it was when we had trainee hired help when Marvin and Glenn were small. It was for 6 months, spring to fall. During the busy spring and harvest time taking meals to the field when working far from home. My folks lived close and were a wonderful help.

8. Were there ever times you felt isolated as a farmwife, or because of living on a farm?

No, there was such a great sense of community.

9. Were there any "new" traditions that you started in your family? (and may have passed down to your children)?

I would say the same traditions from family to family continued on our children. Do the best you can, obey your parents, get your education, respect your elders, have good friends. Enjoy the work you do.

10. Was there anything you were not prepared for, prior to becoming a farmwife?

(Left blank)

11. Were there any expectations of you that proved especially difficult for you?

    (Left blank)

12. Was there anything that you would have liked to (or that you did) change?

    (Left blank)

13. If there was a legacy that you'd like to leave behind from your life here, what would you like it to be? (Such as: your proudest accomplishment, or something important that you instilled in your children)?

    My family - Keep in touch with each other wherever you live. Keep in touch with relations, also with your friends. It is when you get old these relationships mean so much. Be positive - have faith, hope and love. Every day is a blessing.

14. What is your fallback recipe when you're too tired to plan for supper?

    I make my own soups and freeze them. Just warm up or defrost in the microwave and serve. Or have a lasagne in the freezer to thaw.

15. We've all had unexpected guests pop in. What was a trick that you used to ensure you were always prepared for company?

    Muffins or cookies or squares in the freezer. Pop in microwave. Serve muffins with slice of cheese, peanut butter or jam.

16. Do you have any words of advice for women who may be marrying a farmer today?

    Farming is a great family life.

17. What is a key piece of advice you could give to keep a marriage strong?

    Work together, and if you have kids, work together as a family. Take time to spend together … vacations, family trips.

RECIPE FROM EMILY WELSH:
WARMED VEGETABLES ON BREAD:

Warm in microwave: cooked vegetables you have available - cut in cubes: carrots, potatoes, broccoli, yam, cauliflower, onion, parsnips, beets, and pieces of meet (cooked): chicken, beef, etc. Add your favorite spices, tablespoon olive oil, or butter or margarine.

On a microwave plate, put a slice of break or bun halved. Add the warmed cooked vegetables. Top with a slice of cheese and microwave to melt cheese. Add ketchup, if you like.

Great for one or two people depend-
ing on the vegetables you have.

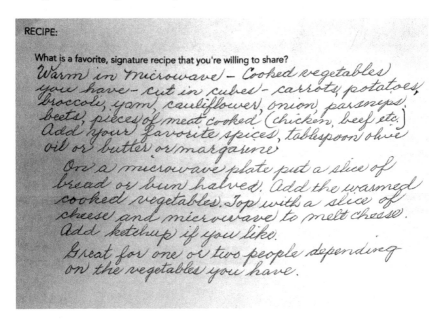

WHAT IS THE IMPACT YOUR MOTHER HAS HAD ON YOUR LIVES?

"Mom was instrumental in instilling attributes of determination, perseverance and commitment in oneself. She showcased this by her endearing love of the farm life and the hard work ethic she embraced during all those years on the farm. She is an amazing lady in her kindness and thoughtfulness of others, and I am a more selfless person because of this. My mom was, and still is, instrumental in instilling a positive outlook on life, and is a motivator to myself to be a good role model to my kids."

By, the children of Emily Welsh

FARMWIFE INTERVIEW #3
Name: Dorothy Wright

Age at this writing: 88

- -

1. How long have you lived in this community?
   Since 1953.

2. What was your background prior to marrying your husband?
   I was from the Mount Joy area and went to Sefton Park School until grade 9. Then, I went to Kitscoty School until grade 12. I had 2 brothers and 1 sister. I am the 3rd in line. I helped supervise school kids in McLaughlin during the teachers strike for 1 year, then south of Vermilion for a year.

3. How long have you been married, and if you have children - how many do you have?
   I married Ralph Wright in July of 1950. We had 2 boys … Darrell and Keith.

4. What has the role of the farmwife meant to you?
   All the inside work … cleaning, cooking, kids. But, I also looked after chickens, milked cows and sold fence posts.

5. What has your husbands' role been?
   Ralph did all the outside farm work. We farmed half a section. He did all the grain harvest.

6. What is the best part, for you, in this life as a farmwife?
   Living on the farm.

7. What is the hardest part?
   Planning a set meal-time! I never knew where they were.

8. Was feeling isolated ever a part of living on the farm? If so, how did you deal with it?
   No … never. You did half of everything anyway so you were rarely alone.

9. Were there any "new" traditions that you started in your family? (and may have passed down to your children)?

Our family was together, but we didn't have money for big holidays. Birthdays, etc. were celebrated, but were not a big deal.

10. Was there anything you were not prepared for, prior to becoming a farmwife?
Having to feed large work crews at the last minute. For example, shinglers.

11. Were there any expectations of you that proved especially difficult for you?
I was from a farm and knew the expectations of me. However, I often had to do more.

12. Was there anything that you would have liked to (or that you did) change?
It was nice when I was able to stop milking cows. When the government ceased egg and milk sales.

13. If there was a legacy that you'd like to leave behind from your life here, what would you like it to be? (Such as: your proudest accomplishment, or something important that you instilled in your children)?
Family photos, memories and security.

14. What is your fallback recipe when you're too tired to plan for supper?
Pancakes and bacon.

15. We've all had unexpected guests pop in. What was a trick that you used to ensure you were always prepared for company?
Baking in the freezer.

16. Do you have any words of advice for women who may be marrying a farmer today?
Teach them to take off their boots at the door, hang their clothes up and don't "plan" for anything!

17. What is a key piece of advice you could give to keep a marriage strong?

My husband passed away in 2007. My advice is to do what you can together, and have hobbies.

RECIPE FROM DOROTHY WRIGHT:
CHOCOLATE CAKE (from Helen Ambler):

Part One:

2 cups white sugar
2/3 cup vegetable oil
2 eggs
2 tsp vanilla

Beat these together well, about 4 minutes.

Part Two:

2 2/3 cups flour
2/3 cup cocoa
2 tsp baking powder
1 tsp salt
2 tsp baking soda

Sift the above ingredients together well, add alternating with 2 cups boiling water, beating well after each addition. Bake at 325C for approximately 50 minutes.

Chocolate Cake (Helen)
1969

2 cups white sugar.
2/3 " veg. oil.
2 eggs.
2 teasp vanilla.
Beat well, about 4 mins.
2 2/3 cups flour.
2/3 cup cocoa.
2 teasp baking powder.
1 " salt
2 " baking soda.
Sift above well to gether, add alternately
with 2 cups boiling water, beating
well after each addition. Bake at
325° for approx. 50 mins.

Dorothea
Wright

FARMWIFE INTERVIEW #4
Name: June Stone

Age at this writing: 79

1. How long have you lived in this community?
   I have lived on the farm for nearly 58 years, but I went to high school in Kitscoty for 2 years.

2. What was your background prior to marrying your husband?
   I was raised on a farm near Marwayne, AB. I attended a country school and Marwayne School before taking grade 11 and 12 in Kitscoty and living in a dormitory. Then, I spent a year helping my parents on the family farm. I met Bob in high school at 17 years old.

3. How long have you been married, and if you have children - how many do you have?
   As of June 30, 2015, Bob and I will be married for 60 years. We married in 1955. I was 18. We have 4 children, 1 son and 3 daughters. We have 6 grandchildren and 1 great grandchild.

4. What has the role of the farmwife meant to you?
   It has meant unstructured time with family and friends, working and playing with family, and the freedom to enjoy nature.

5. What has your husbands' role been?
   He "thought" he was the boss (CEO).

6. What is the best part, for you, in this life as a farmwife?
   All the things in #4. Working with my partner.

7. What is the hardest part?
   Accepting some of the changes. Two years ago, we left the farm and moved to town - it's been a hard transition. I miss the quietness and the kids coming in and out.

8. Was feeling isolated ever a part of living on the farm? If so, how did you deal with it?
   Probably when I had small children. Mostly, I think you dealt with it by being busy. I can remember once when the kids were small, one of my girls dropped a glass and the other

stepped it in. She was bleeding. It wasn't easy to just pop into town, so I just had to deal with it. I bet she still has a scar.

9. Were there any "new" traditions that you started in your family? (and, may have passed down to your children)?

Watching and feeding the wild birds. Trying to get the whole family together for a holiday every year.

10. Was there anything you were not prepared for, prior to becoming a farmwife?

That I didn't always know where my husband was working. When a community member Daryl Davidson was injured, it really scared a lot of us. I know a lot of wives worried about not knowing where our husbands were if they needed help.

11. Were there any expectations of you that proved especially difficult for you?

Learning to live so close to Bob's family.

12. Was there anything that you would have liked to (or that you did) change?

They finally started to tell me where they were working after a few long walks when equipment broke down.

13. If there was a legacy that you'd like to leave behind from your life here, what would you like it to be? (Such as: your proudest accomplishment, or something important that you instilled in your children)?

Proudest accomplishment: that my kids (now grown-ups) have said "thank you for being there for us when we were growing up".

14. What is your fallback recipe when you're too tired to plan for supper?

Let the guys do the cooking! This has really come about after the death of my sister-in-law and watching her husband struggle to feed himself.

15. We've all had unexpected guests pop in. What was a trick that you used to ensure you were always prepared for company?

A few goodies stashed in the freezer, or more recently, crackers, cheese, veggies and dip (and garlic sausage for the guys).

16. Do you have any words of advice for women who may be marrying a farmer today?

Be flexible - don't expect too much - but keep your independence. You have to work at your marriage so take time to have fun andrelaxation with the farmer! And, don't "start" doing something you wouldn't want to continue doing for your life (or marriage)!

17. What is a key piece of advice you could give to keep a marriage strong?

A lot of give and take. Don't let things bother you. Do things together … Bob says: even when you may not have wanted to.

RECIPE FROM JUNE STONE:
SLOW COOKER STEW:

My slow cooker is one of my favorite appliances. I use it for stew, soup and pot roasts! Just put vegetables and meat in the morning, turn it on and forget about it until supper.

I usually put onions and carrots in the bottom and then the meat with potatoes around the meat. Season with pepper and salt and whatever grabs you. You can use other vegetables and tomatoes if you wish (or whatever you have).

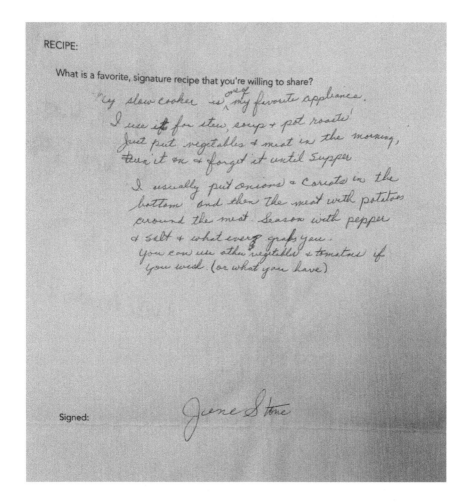

RECIPE:

What is a favorite, signature recipe that you're willing to share?

"My slow cooker is over my favorite appliance.
I use it for stew, soup + pot roast!
Just put vegetables + meat in the morning,
turn it on + forget it until supper
    I usually put onions + carrots in the
bottom and then the meat with potatoes
around the meat. Season with pepper
+ salt + what ever grabs you.
You can use other vegetables + tomatoes if
you wish. (or what you have)

Signed: *June Stone*

WHAT IS THE IMPACT YOUR MOTHER HAS HAD ON YOUR LIVES?

"We look back now and realize how lucky we were to have grown up on a farm in rural Alberta. Our mother may not have had a "get out there and get paid" kind of a job but she did have the most important job of all - raising 4 children. She wore many hats on any given day. Whether it was the taxi driver, catering truck, accountant, psychologist, educator, gardener, chef, maid, care giver or just mom - she was always there when we needed her. Over the past 20 years we have seen what other people consider family life. We now look back and realize how lucky we were to have been so well taken care of by both our mother and father, as well as, by our grand parents who lived in the same yard. We never went hungry because we had livestock and gardens. We always had clothes, whether they were new, hand me downs, or something mom sewed. And we always had a roof over our heads. These basic needs, and being loved everyday of our lives - even as adults - is more than some people ever get. Thanks to our mom for being who you are and treating us the way you knew we deserved to be treated - just as the saying goes: "treat others the way you want to be treated". So, on that note, she taught us about: respect, hard work, understanding and caring.

If she needed something done, she just did it. If she needed something grown, she planted it. If she needed something made, she just made it, and so on. Mom never asked too many questions, she just got the job done - whatever it was. We became strong, confident and independent individuals just from the beliefs and values taught to us by our mother."

By, the children of June Stone

FARMWIFE INTERVIEW #5
Name: Linda Amundrud

Linda Amundrud heading back out to complete morning chores after our interview in December of 2014. Age at this writing: 58

1. How long have you lived in this community?

I've lived in the Hillmond/Tangleflags community for over 36 years.

2. What was your background prior to marrying your husband?

I have been involved with farming my whole life, so 58 years. I grew up on a cattle ranch at Frenchman's Butte, about 15 miles north across the river. After graduating from Paradise Hill School, I moved to Lloydminster for a few years to work. This is where I met my husband. Oddly enough, he told me he liked my Camaro Rally Sport, but I guess it was more than just the car he had a liking for, as it was the start of a long relationship.

3. How long have you been married, and if you have children - how many do you have?

I married my husband Don in October, 1978. Shortly after settling into the farm life, we started a family. In 1980, our first daughter Amanda was born. In 1981, Dean was born, Last but not least, our youngest daughter Lindsey was born in 1983. Today, we have the greatest pleasure of all, as we get to carry on the tradition, of being grandparents. This truly is the best gift your children can share with you. We currently have 3 grandsons, and 2 granddaughters, and always hoping for more.

4. What has the role of the farmwife meant to you?

My role on the farm, was to pretty much tackle any chore that needed to be done at the time, whether it was milking cows, calving, seeding or taking the crop off. There is always lots of work to be done, and an extra set of hands is very helpful. Don and I both worked off the farm, when we first got married. I worked in Lloydminster, about 25 miles away, and Don, worked in the oil patch. My parents gave us a milk cow, for a Wedding gift, so I had to milk the cow before going to work. This lasted for a couple of years, until we started having a family, and I couldn't fit under the cow anymore.

5. What has your husbands' role been?

Don's dream when we got married, was that he would work off the farm for five years, to get the farm established, then just farm. Unfortunately we have been married 36 years, and Don, still hasn't "just farmed". Having said that, we wouldn't have been able to build up the farm, and continue to enjoy the farm life as we do without that extra income. I've always said that, "Don works out, so I can keep farming". We are a great team, we work well together, and seem to be on the same page almost, all of the time. We feel very lucky, to have been able to purchase the Amundrud Family farm, that was homesteaded by Don's grandparents from Norway, in 1909. They suffered many hardships, but enjoyed a much simpler life style.

6. What is the best part, for you, in this life as a farmwife?

The best part of being a farmwife is that every day you can have something different to do. You get to plant your garden, and watch it grow. You make pies from the apples you pick from your own trees. I love calving season, even though you have had very little sleep, watching the baby calves get their first drink, or bottle feeding the twins, so they have a good start. Nothing beats the grand children coming over helping to clean the barn, and help feed the baby calves. They get the pleasure of seeing life begin, as they experience birth of new born calves, or just trying to tame the new born kittens.

7. What is the hardest part?

Life, really is good on the farm, but it does come with its challenges. I can remember, when we first got married, and had a young family, wondering if we would ever see an end to all the bills. There never was a lot of money, but you always had lots of potatoes, your own meat, and a cold room full of canning, and the freezer full of vegetables. We never went hungry, and enjoyed what nature had helped us to harvest. My kids always laugh, because if they need to make something, they come to Mom's grocery store, because the pantry is always well stocked. We always seem to have enough, that we could survive at least a couple of weeks of blocked roads, without needing to go to the store. After being used to feeding a family, now that we are empty nesters, it is hard to cook for only two.

8. Was feeling isolated ever a part of living on the farm? If so, how did you deal with it?

I would have to say that I never felt isolated, even though in winter we could be blocked in for three to four days, until the roads were opened again. We had lots of neighbors close by, and we always had the coffee on, so seemed to have someone coming or going most days. I was also fortunate to have most of my family close by, which gave a sense of security.

9. Were there any "new" traditions that you started in your family? (and may have passed down to your children)?

One of our new family traditions, we have started in the past few years is very dear to our hearts. In 2009 we celebrated 100 years since our farm was homesteaded. To help commemorate the event, we moved a log cabin on to the home quarter. A cousin from BC, had the original Amundrud cook stove, and wanted it to come back to the farm. Long story short, we drove to Golden, B.C., picked up the 90 year old cook stove, and got it totally restored. Now, we can enjoy baking bread, buns or stews, on the old stove, and have family gatherings in the cabin. There isn't many things that last 90 years, and work as good as it did when it was new. Many memories, and many hands have cooked on that old Amundrud stove. Lots of family members brought back Amundrud treasures, and wanted them displayed in the cabin, so we now keep our heritage alive, for the next generation to enjoy. The grandkids enjoy the fire pit, marsh mellows, and wiener roasts. It is our little piece of heaven, and Don and I enjoy walking to the cabin, have a crib game, and spend the night, with no power , and no outside influences, just the sounds of silence. It is so peaceful.

Another family tradition is doing puzzles at Christmas time. Everyone enjoys sitting down and visiting, while working on a puzzle. We do at least 2 to 3 puzzles every year, and always look forward to the next season. The little guys do their own age appropriate puzzles, so they get to be part of the tradition, enjoying the laughter, and family time.

10. Was there anything you were not prepared for, prior to becoming a farmwife?

I wasn't prepared for all the hard work and certain expectations that are put on farm women. You had to always have a clean house, even though you were outside tending to chores or looking after a huge garden. I had no idea how much work there was on the farm, even though I was raised as a farm girl. My mother made everything look easy, not realizing she probably never got hardly any sleep. I came from a family of eight kids, so you can imagine wash day, when they did it all by hand. We all had jobs at a young age, which must have helped Mom and Dad over the years.

I have a funny memory as a young girl proving you should never, say never. I was raised on a farm, so we knew all about hard work, at a very young age. I always said, "I would never marry a farmer". I knew how hard you had to work, and coming from a big family, I knew there wasn't a lot of money. Now looking back, we always had fun, we rode horses, built forts in the pasture, ate homemade ice cream, life was great. As a newlywed, starting to farm, it was very different. All the jobs had to be done by only the two of you.

11. Were there any expectations of you that proved especially difficult for you?

When we first got married, we spent about six months with my husband's parents at the farm, where they had lived for the past 30 years. I didn't feel, that I was prepared to share the kitchen, with my new mother in law, as I wanted to impress my husband with my cooking skills. Now looking back, I realize how hard it would have been for my mother in law to share her territory. We are not taught how to be good daughter in laws, and our mother in laws are still learning how to deal with more family members, both trying to do what is right. I was very fortunate to have good in laws, as I sure didn't plan on living with them, when I was a new bride.

As a young farmers wife, you always had to be prepared to drop whatever you were doing to go help them, you are on call 24-7, but I never minded because you had a partnership, and you learned to work and laugh together, you were a great team.

12. Was there anything that you would have liked to (or that you did) change?

We spent a lot of time and effort to make our yard and farm our own. As our land along the river was more adapt to raising cattle, and as a reflection of my love for animals, we built corrals, lots of new fencing, and slowly converted to a cattle operation from grain farming. Our hip roof barn was built in 1928, and hadn't been painted for many years, with a few coats of paint and a new roof, it stands as proud as it did 85 years ago. Our old chicken house was also given a face-lift, and a new roof, as it was the first building on the farm. My granddaughter, Eva' said "Grandma, why do you always call it the chicken house? You don't even have any chickens". It is actually the wood-shed now, but was used as the first house, then a chicken house. We strive to maintain at least some of the heritage of the farm, and are sure that Grandpa and Grandma Amundrud would be very pleased to look down and see how well it has been maintained over the years.

13. If there was a legacy that you'd like to leave behind from your life here, what would you like it to be? (Such as: your proudest accomplishment, or something important that you instilled in your children)?

I guess if there is any legacy that I could leave to my children and family would be my apple pie recipe. I want to know that I have taught my kids and the grandkids the technique to making my renowned pie crust, that was handed down to me when I was 13 years old, by my mother who was a very good cook. I get great pleasure from making pies, tarts and pastry baking. My sister in law Marion, and I usually get together and make enough pies and tarts to last the next year for both households, and we do love our sweets. We were fortunate enough to get nearly 40 apple pies from our own apple tree this year. There is always great pleasure and satisfaction, when you are complimented on your cooking ability, and fortunately my husband always says how much he enjoyed the meal. I think it is because as they say, "the way to a man's heart is through his stomach".

14. What is your fallback recipe when you're too tired to plan for supper?

A "woman's work is never done", and this reminds me of a time when I had been out baling all day, and my husband came home from working in town, and asked what was on the menu. Again, I through very clear and explicit explanation, told him that perhaps he could have brought something from town to the field. Now there is usually food in the field if he is coming home from work in town. I guess that all goes back to that team effort, and a little give and take.

15. We've all had unexpected guests pop in. What was a trick that you used to ensure you were always prepared for company?

If you have unexpected guests, I advise all young wives to always have some hamburger in your deep freeze. You can whip up a pot of chili, or hamburger soap, or stew in no time. Being most farm wives have a big garden, there will be no lack of potatoes or vegetables, which will feed a lot of mouths. I always love to can some fruit in the fall, so if you add ice cream, and a cookie, makes a great and very simple dessert.

16. Do you have any words of advice for women who may be marrying a farmer today?

My advice to any young woman that is marrying a farmer today, would be to enjoy every day you get to spend outside while working side by side with your husband, whether you are feeding cows, fencing, planting garden, or harvesting. Yes, we get to help lots, and learn lots without much training, and sometimes feel unappreciated, but at the end of the day we are our own boss. Our children get to feel the dirt between their toes, learn how to work, learn about life, and usually learn how to drive long before they are old enough. Enjoy working with your husband, as a partner, that will give you satisfaction, and the sense of ownership to what you are doing and what you have built together. The farm is such a wonderful place to raise your family.

I truly believe it is very important to respect our mother in laws challenges and remember, we are marrying their babies, and I always say no one will love your child like a parent does. We have to be patient and earn our spot on the ladder, one rung at a time.

17. What is a key piece of advice you could give to keep a marriage strong?

I truly believe in order to keep your marriage strong, you both have to learn to listen. You have to believe in each other, show compassion to each other, and have complete trust in each other. Be kind to one another, but also have a voice. Your opinion is important, and matters, but show respect to each other. I feel as you get older you learn to appreciate each other for who you are and what you represent. Don't try to change who you are, or who your spouse is. Remember you were both raised in different households, but you have to appreciate what values you both may have. You truly do become best friends, and you learn that a simple hug and a kiss goes a long way in keeping your marriage alive. Never go to bed angry, and be sure to say you are "sorry". Life is too short to worry about the small things, they will look after themselves. Every day we must be grateful for the life we have been given, and try to do something nice for someone else. Remember when you get up in the morning, you can decide if you want to have a good day or a bad day. Keep smiling, and have lots of laughter.

I always find if I'm having a not such a good day, I would enjoy a visit with one of my old and dear neighbors. My one friend just turned 102 years old on Dec 12. You could never forget her birthday as she born on 12/12/12. We would get together and talk about our cows, or cutting hay. She always knew how to lift up your day. We would go out and chop some wood, so she could start up the old cook stove to make a coffee. She only knew how to cook on a wood stove. The Seniors Center never knew what a gem they were about to get when Isabel left the farm at the age of 95. She was still actively farming, and had a few cows to feed every day. Isabel taught me a lot about farming, as she was widowed, and farmed on her own for 35 years. She taught me a lot about enjoying all the simple things in life. We would go berry picking, so she could make a Saskatoon pie on the old cook stove. Her last berry-picking trip was when she was last living on the farm at 95 years.

Never take anything for granted, we are only on this earth for a short time, so make the best of it. Enjoy every day, as we live in a beautiful country, and have all the freedom to do whatever we put our minds to. We feel very blessed to continue to farm the land and reap the harvest that it gives us.

RECIPE FROM LINDA AMUNDRUD:
PASTRY:

1 lb tenderflake lard (cold from the fridge)
1 tsp salt
1 tsp baking powder
4 cups Robin Hood flour

Work this until crumbly.

In a ¾ cup measuring cup, beat: 1 egg, add 1
tbsp vinegar and fill with ice cold water.

Mix the liquid with your crumb mixture, work into a ball and
roll when you're ready to make a beautiful homemade pie.

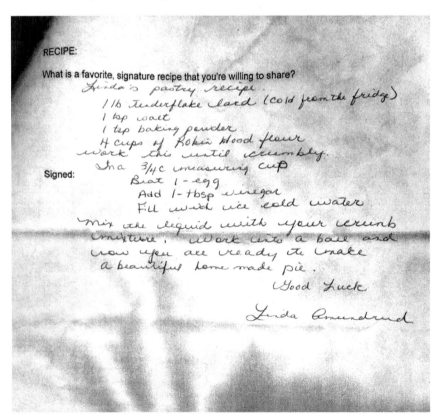

WHAT IS THE IMPACT YOUR MOTHER HAS HAD ON YOUR LIVES?

"Mom is an example of self-motivation and discipline. She teaches us it is possible to wake up each day, choose to smile, and go out to work for something one loves. It is absolute intrinsic motivation. The animals don't seem to offer a direct level of encouragement - although it is obvious there is some sort of exchange of gratitude! Mom has taught us the understanding of duality. She has shown how to be a physically strong woman with a powerful mind and a soft, loving heart. She has hands that help to pull new calves, carry heavy loads, and drive equipment. Those same hands keep our family nurtured with homemade meals and pies, gardens of flowers, fresh grown food and a lifetime of gentle hugs. She is grounded and connected to the land. She inspires us to listen and soften into our instincts. She is confident and hilarious. She is a model of speaking ones truth, practicing forgiveness and knowing when to draw a line in the sand. She encourages us to laugh and take time to play. She teaches empathy and reminds us the she is only ever as happy as her child in the most pain. She holds us in her heart and has taught us what eternal, unconditional love of a mother is."

By, the children of Linda Amundrud

FARMWIFE INTERVIEW #6
Name: Verna Presley

Age at this writing: 89

- -

1. How long have you lived in this community?

     I lived in the Wildwood Community since 1957.

2. What was your background prior to marrying your husband?

     I was born on March 29, 1926 on my grandparents' farm north of Maidstone, SK and then moved home with my parents to their farm in the Standard Hill District further north of Maidstone not far from the North Saskatchewan River. My brother Gale was born in February 1928, and soon after, my dad died of a type of blood cancer in June, 1928. I still remember my dad playing with me, flipping me in the kitchen and I missed him all of my life. I know that my life would have been much different had he lived to love us. My mother remarried and I have three half sisters. My step dad was a workaholic and everyone else had to work with no play unless we snuck away. We all worked hard and I went to school at Eldon country school up to Grade 8 and then I was going to quit school. Some of my Mothers' relatives caught wind of this and took me to live with them at Kerrobert, SK and I took my Grade 9. My step-father and mother purchased the store at Bartel Sk and we moved up there in 1944. My step-father went away to work up north and Mom ran the store but I was the delivery person, hauling cream and freight so that was hard work too. My step-father passed away in 1945 so my mother and all of us moved back to north of Maidstone to be closer to her brothers. Eventually we moved into Maidstone and I worked at the local grocery store until I was married. I was married on November 1, 1947.

3. How long have you been married, and if you have children - how many do you have?

     I was married 47 years and then separated. Gene passed away in May 2012. We had 6 children four girls, Marilyn, Diane, Karen and Ronda and then two boys Kevin and Darwin. We have 14 grandchildren and two great great grandchildren, at present. I love them all, but are all different in their own way. Most of all, they are healthy,   and enjoying life.

4. What has the role of the farmwife meant to you?

I loved being a farmwife and part of mixed farming operation and raising our children on the farm. I took pride in all I did and always did a good job of everything. I had to be prepared for anything and at any time but no different than most farm women at that time. I would keep my house, washing, gardening, food ready and always raised at least 100 chickens to butcher for meat and then I worked outside all year round. I milked lots of cows, helped calve the cows out, work on the tractor cultivating, harrowing, baling, drove truck at sileage time, hauled the grain and of course we didn't have a hoist on the truck so had to shovel it all off, operated the swather and combine as well. Then as any farmwife who worked outside there was my work to do when I got back into the house. Not many men were taught how to do the women's work (haha). I was very lucky that I had my kids as they all learned to work wherever needed. When my kids were older I went to work at a hotel in Lloydminster. Farm life was too much for me by then.

5. What has your husbands' role been?

My husband did a lot of work on the farm as well. His mother and father helped us with all the farm duties until they weren't able to do it anymore. There were many things that my husband and I didn't agree on, one being that you didn't go away and enjoy things unless all the work was done first. Looking back if we had worked together on getting the work done up then we would have gone and enjoyed life more often. We both loved to fish but most often I had to stay home with the children or finish work that wasn't done up. I think that many of times it was my choice to stay home and try to get caught up.

6. What is the best part, for you, in this life as a farmwife?

I think that raising my children on the farm and teaching my boys how to run the implements, work with the cattle, and my girls to keep a clean house and be able to cook a meal. I was proud of all my kids and we had fun working together.

7. What is the hardest part?

I think the hardest part for me was all the hard work and long hours. I worked so hard that really didn't take time to enjoy life. I would do it so much different if I had a second chance. I would take time to smell the roses and enjoy everything that I did. It is easy to say that now but at the time when you are trying to make a living for yourself and family, keep the bills all paid up it is hard to smell the roses. I would try to manage things so that the work was not so hard and the hours not so long.

8. Was feeling isolated ever a part of living on the farm? If so, how did you deal with it?

I never felt isolated on the farm. I was busy all day with my chores etc. and in the evening I liked to play my accordion most nights my kids would go to sleep to the music. I also crocheted, knit, sewed, and liked to play cards. I loved my music most of all and it was a comfort to me. I played by ear so would just pick up my accordion and play. My brother and I were playing for dances when we were 10 and 12. Ride our horses to the country hall and then play for hours and ride home again. That was fun! Playing by ear is a gift that you never loose. I can't remember how our instruments got to the old hall but someone must have picked them up. I still play my organ and love all the old time music. We had many friends that would drop for a visit and my brother's family and ours spend a lot of time together playing cards and having fun.

9. Were there any "new" traditions that you started in your family? (and may have passed down to your children)?

I taught my children be to ready for what ever hits you. My gift of music did not pass down to any of my children but some of my grandchildren have the gift of music. I tried to pass on to my children that they should get together often and always get along as life is too short to be apart. Always be there for one another.

10. Was there anything you were not prepared for, prior to becoming a farmwife?
I learned to work hard at a very young age so I was prepared for that but would have liked to been able to get the work all done up and take time to enjoy everything more. I never was able to sit and enjoy when there was work to be done. When we married we had nothing so were buying land, cattle and machinery so we had to work hard in order to keep our lively hood going.

11. Were there any expectations of you that proved especially difficult for you?
I was always very afraid of heights. Climbing the ladder to put the lids on the granaries terrified me.
I never enjoyed being alone at night and through out my life it seemed that I was. At first I was very nervous operating all the implements but got used of that the more I did.

12. Was there anything that you would have liked to (or that you did) change?
If doing it again I would get to know my partner better before getting married and think about all the responsibility that comes with making a living and having a family. I really think that I would still love to make my life on the farm.
I should have thought things over more before I got married.

13. If there was a legacy that you'd like to leave behind from your life here, what would you like it to be? (Such as: your proudest accomplishment, or something important that you instilled in your children)?

I'm proud of what I've done. I don't know if I did it all right, but I did a lot. I did a good job with my kids and I'm very proud of all of them. I think that I would pass along to always do everything right the first time around. I am proud of all my family and friends, and all the music I have played in my 89 years.

14. What is your fallback recipe when you're too tired to plan for supper?

Canned chicken or made a thick soup with veggies, water, rice and chicken.

15. We've all had unexpected guests pop in. What was a trick that you used to ensure you were always prepared for company?

I always had canned meat in my vegetable room, lots of potatoes, frozen vegetables. I would on many occasions go and butcher one or two of the tasty home raised chickens and everyone enjoyed fried chicken with cream gravy. I usually had canned fruit and could find some sweets around. We used to have lots of company and those were good times. Or, toast and jam. Ha Ha!

16. Do you have any words of advice for women who may be marrying a farmer today?

I would tell them not to get too smart around the machinery and then you would have more time to enjoy your inside work. Women are not built to do heavy work and take those rough rides around the fields. You will suffer in your golden years if you work too hard when young.

17. What is a key piece of advice you could give to keep a marriage strong?

I would say you must marry your best friend and enjoy things together. Praise one another not criticize. Plan your work so that you have some time to relax and enjoy and always respect one another and be able to trust one another.

Do things together.

RECIPE FROM VERNA PRESLEY:
MY BUN RECIPE:

It goes as follows;

6 cups of hot water
2 Tablespoons of salt 1⁄2 cup of margarine 1⁄4 cup of oil

Mix well and add 6 cups of flour and mix
well and let cool off somewhat.

In a small bowl put 3⁄4 of warm water, 1 tablespoon of sugar, and 2 heaping tablespoons of
yeast. Stir up and let stand for 10 minutes.

By this time your flour mixture should be cool
enough to add the yeast and water. Mix well!

Add another 6 cups of flour.
Mix and knead well and put into a large bowl.

Let rise in a warm place such as your oven with light
on for about 3⁄4 of an hour, double in size.

Punch down and let rise again and put in pans. Let rise
double in size and bake at 400 for 20 minutes or whatever
time your oven needs to make the buns cooked and brown.

Butter tops of buns with a pastry brush and remove from pan
onto a rack to let them cool. This should make about 60 buns.

MY BUN RECIPE

It goes as follows;

6 cups of hot water
2 Tablespoons of salt
½ cup of margarine
¼ cup of oil

Mix well and add 6 cups of flour and mix well and let cool off somewhat.

In a small bowl put ¾ of warm water, 1 tablespoon of sugar, and 2 heaping tablespoons of yeast. Stir up and let stand for 10 minutes.

By this time your flour mixture should be cool enough to add the yeast and water. Mix well!

Add another 6 cups of flour.

Mix and knead well and put into a large bowl.

Let rise in a warm place such as your oven with light on for about ¾ of an hour, double in size.

Punch down and let rise again and put in pans. Let rise double in size and bake at 400 for 20 minutes or whatever time your oven needs to make the buns cooked and brown.

Butter tops of buns with a pastry brush and remove from pan onto a rack to let them cool.

This should make about 60 buns.

Verna Presley

WHAT IS THE IMPACT YOUR MOTHER HAS HAD ON YOUR LIVES?

"I would first like to mention that our Mother worked hard and always had us kids first in her mind. I learned to cook, clean, accept responsibility, to tell the truth, be honest, to always do my best at the first try in what I did and much more. My Mom was a perfectionist and most time made her life hard and miserable because of it. I have learned over the years to do all these things but to take time to enjoy and be proud of what I have done. My husband and I have worked together with hard work and also time to travel, enjoy and relax. I passed all the qualities that I learned from my mother onto my children and now my grandchildren. I am the oldest child of Verna, Marilyn Yvonne Hougham, married Thomas Hougham on January 6, 1968. We had two children, and have two grandsons. Nothing is better than be a GRANDMOTHER!!!!!!!"

By, Marilyn Hougham, daughter of Verna Presley

FARMWIFE INTERVIEW #7
Name: Elaine Quinn

Age at this writing: 59

1. How long have you lived in this community?
   37 years.

2. What was your background prior to marrying your husband?
   Town girl, had relatives that farmed, but had no real experience.

3. How long have you been married, and if you have children - how many do you have?
   37 years, and 2 kids.

4. What has the role of the farmwife meant to you?
   Raising kids, keeping house and cooking, baking, canning. Working spring and fall helping Jim ie. cultivating, harrowing, hauling grain. Being at his beck and call whenever he needed help. ie. Fencing, repairing, running to town.

5. What has your husbands' role been?
   Helping with the kids when he had time ie. not working. Running the farm, doing farm books.

6. What is the best part, for you, in this life as a farmwife?
   Spending time with Jim, working with him, going with him on farm business. Being part of a team.

7. What is the hardest part?
   Spending time with Jim, ei. helping with farm equipment and repairs. Going to things for the kid alone because he was always "busy" ie. farming.

8. Was feeling isolated ever a part of living on the farm? If so, how did you deal with it?
   No, I never felt isolated. By the time we were married, we were going into Lloyd at least once a week. Also, because I drove I could go wherever I wanted whenever I wanted. It was different for the older ladies who didn't drive when they were young.

9. Were there any "new" traditions that you started in your family? (and may have passed down to your children)?

Christmas morning and holidays. Holidays in Jim's family were not real important.

10. Was there anything you were not prepared for, prior to becoming a farmwife?

Big learning curve, learning to drive farm trucks and tractors. Fewer holidays, no such thing as long weekends. Weekends were just more work.

11. Were there any expectations of you that proved especially difficult for you?

Feeling I couldn't do some things because I had to look after the kids - Jim was busy with the farm. Feeling the farm was more important than us.

12. Was there anything that you would have liked to (or that you did) change?

See above. Has improved, but "work and farm" are still the most important things in life. One thing I did change was taking morning and then afternoon coffee to the field. They could take it with them.

13. If there was a legacy that you'd like to leave behind from your life here, what would you like it to be? (Such as: your proudest accomplishment, or something important that you instilled in your children)?

I think just be proud of a job well done, do your best and work for a living, but take time for yourself.

14. What is your fallback recipe when you're too tired to plan for supper?

Macaroni and cheese or macaroni with bacon and tomatoes.

15. We've all had unexpected guests pop in. What was a trick that you used to ensure you were always prepared for company?

Usually had something you could pull out of the deep freeze.

16. Do you have any words of advice for women who may be marrying a farmer today?
Be prepared to work hard, it still isn't an easy life. Be prepared for the stress of poor weather, crops, prices and be supportive.

17. What is a key piece of advice you could give to keep a marriage strong?
Being together physically, i.e.. working together, spending time together as a family but also just the two of you; being together mentally, share the same dreams and wishes. When all is said and done and I've complained and bitched, I'd still rather spend time with Jim than anyone else!

RECIPE FROM ELAINE QUINN:
Meatballs and Gravy (which I learned from his mother - Gladys):

1 pound ground beef

1 egg

4 heaping tbsp bread crumbs
1 heaping tsp allspice

salt and pepper to taste

Mix together and form into meatballs (which I flatten slightly)

Brown and remove form pan. Add oil if needed to pan, add flour to oil
and mix til moistened. Add potato water gradually to make gravy. Add half can of mushroom soup and add water to

desired consistency. Add meatballs
back to pan and simmer.

Mash potatoes with creamed cheese and milk.

Buttered beets

Cheesecake (everyone's favorite):

1 cup crushed graham wafers
1/2 tsp cinnamon

2 tbsp sugar

1/4 cup margarine
Combine and press into a 9 inch pan
250 g pkg cream cheese
1/2 cup sugar

1 tbsp lemon juice

1 tsp lemon rind (optional)
1 tsp vanilla

Mix together:

Whip 1/2 cup of whipping cream with
sugar and vanilla.

Combine with cream cheese mixture and pour over crust.

Cover with cherry or blueberry pie filling.

(Thickened and sweetened frozen blueberries
seasoned with cinnamon are our favorite)

Meatballs and Gravy (which I learned from his mother – Gladys Q.)

1 pound ground beef
1 egg
4 heaping tbsp bread crumbs
1 heaping tsp allspice
salt and pepper to taste

Mix together and form into meatballs (which I flatten slightly)
Brown and remove form pan. Add oil if needed to pan, add flour to oil
and mix til moistened. Add potato water gradually to make gravy. Add half can
of mushroom soup and add water to desired consistency. Add meatballs
back to pan and simmer.

Mash potatoes with creamed cheese and milk.

Buttered beets

Cheesecake (everyone's fave)

1 cup crushed graham wafers
1/2 tsp cinnamon
2 tbsp sugar
1/4 cup margarine
Combine and press into a 9 inch pan

250 g pkg cream cheese
1/2 cup sugar
1 tbsp lemon juice
1 tsp lemon rind (optional)
1 tsp vanilla
Mix together

Whip 1/2 cup of whipping cream with
sugar and vanilla.
Combine with cream cheese mixture and pour
over crust.

Cover with cherry or blueberry pie filling.
(Thickened and sweetened frozen blueberries
seasoned with cinnamon are our favorite)

** Elaine Quinn

FARMWIFE INTERVIEW #8
Name: Marilyn Mitchell

Age at this writing: 62

- -

1. How long have you lived in this community?

    I grew up down the road in Blackfoot. After getting married 44 years ago I have been a part of the Kitscoty community.

2. What was your background prior to marrying your husband?

    I graduated from Kitscoty High School, worked for 1 year at the Border Credit Union in Lloydminster, then we were married and I became a farm girl.

3. How long have you been married, and if you have children - how many do you have?

    Les and I have been married almost 44 years, and very proud to say we have 5 wonderful children: Jason, Billie Jo, Becky, Tyson and Lindsey. With their partners they have blessed us with, at present, 11 beautiful grandchildren.

4. What has the role of the farmwife meant to you?

    As a farmwife, I have tried to do my part to make our farm successful. Initially, my most important task was raising our children. As they grew older, I was able to help with more jobs on the farm. I have always been the farm bookkeeper and enjoy doing that. My Kubota lawn mower has been my main piece of equipment, love doing yard work.

5. What has your husbands' role been?

    Les has always been the chief decision maker on our farm, at first with guidance from his dad, and now with help from our Son. He worked hard to provide a comfortable lifestyle for our growing family. He taught our children to love the land and nature, to treat it with respect and in turn it would reward you with a sense of pride and accomplishment.

6. What is the best part, for you, in this life as a farmwife?

    There are so many "best parts" to being a farmwife. I feel so lucky to have been able to stay home and raise our children, working alongside Les to provide a safe home environment. The smell of fresh cut hay, newborn calves bucking and playing, picnics at the river pasture with family, life as a farm-wife is the best.

7. What is the hardest part?

I feel the hardest part is dealing with the stress. I know I worry too much, but in agriculture there are so many ups and downs, drought, BSE and the list goes on. I had to learn to handle the stress so it did not affect our family life.

8. Was feeling isolated ever a part of living on the farm? If so, how did you deal with it?

No, I never felt isolated as we were not far from Kitscoty and we had family close by.

9. Were there any "new" traditions that you started in your family? (and may have passed down to your children)?

Our family does not really have any traditions. We all loved my grandmothers' Swedish hard tack or thin bread, my Mom started coming to help me make it each Christmas, and now I am teaching my girls to make it. I guess you would call it a new tradition I am passing on to my children.

10. Was there anything you were not prepared for, prior to becoming a farmwife?

I can't thick of anything I was not prepared for except the long days of work that Les put in.

11. Were there any expectations of you that proved especially difficult for you?

No expectations. Everyone was patient with me as I was not raised on a farm. I had to learn about farming, I was lucky to be part of a family of wonderful mentors.

12. Was there anything that you would have liked to (or that you did) change?

I wish we had taken more family holidays. Work on the farm never ends but family time is important.

13. If there was a legacy that you'd like to leave behind from your life here, what would you like it to be? (Such as: your proudest accomplishment, or something important that you instilled in your children)?

Get involved in your community, volunteer and help make projects happen. Don't sit back and complain about why needs to be done, pitch in and do your own little part.

14. What is your fallback recipe when you're too tired to plan for supper?

Soup and sandwiches (tomato soup and grilled cheese is a favorite) or wieners and kraft dinner.

15. We've all had unexpected guests pop in. What was a trick that you used to ensure you were always prepared for company?

My freezer is always well stocked and it is a standing joke in our family that I could feed everyone for a year with my cluttered cold room, home canning, cases of soup, sugar, flour and all the necessities.

16. Do you have any words of advice for women who may be marrying a farmer today?

Farming has changed so much in the past few years, but still requires dedication and hard work. Support your partner and offer suggestions. You will be rewarded with a lifestyle like no other.

17. What is a key piece of advice you could give to keep a marriage strong?

Support your partner through the good and the bad, always be there for one another. Be sure to make time to enjoy each others company.

RECIPE FROM MARILYN MITCHELL:
FARMERS' MEATLOAF:

"My dad's favorite meal was meatloaf, so this is my Mom's recipe. A favorite with all of our family" – Marilyn Mitchell.

- 2 lb ground beef
- 2 eggs slightly beaten
- ½ cup dry bread crumbs
- 1 cup milk
- ½ cup grated onion
- ½ tsp salt
- ¼ tsp pepper
- 1 tsp sage

Sauce:

- 3 tbsp brown sugar
- 4 tbsp ketchup
- ¼ tsp nutmeg
- 1 tsp dry mustard

Directions:

Soak breadcrumbs in milk. Add remaining ingredients, pack lightly in a greased loaf pan. Spread sauce on top. Bake at 350C for 1 ¼ hours. Enjoy!

RECIPE:

What is a favorite, signature recipe that you're willing to share?

My dad's favorite meal was meatloaf so this is mom's recipe for meatloaf. A favorite with all our family.

FARMERS MEATLOAF

2 # GROUND BEEF
2 EGGS SLIGHTLY BEATEN
½ CUP DRY BREAD CRUMBS
1 CUP MILK
½ CUP GRATED ONION
½ TSP SALT.
¼ TSP PEPPER
1 TSP SAGE.

SAUCE
3 TBSP BROWN SUGAR
4 TBSP KETCHUP
¼ TSP NUTMEG
1 TSP DRY MUSTARD

SOAK BREADCRUMBS IN MILK. ADD REMAINING INGREDIENTS, PACK LIGHTLY IN A GREASED LOAF PAN. SPREAD SAUCE ON TOP. BAKE AT 350° FOR 1¼ HRS. ENJOY!

Signed: Marilyn Mitchell

WHAT IS THE IMPACT YOUR MOTHER HAS HAD ON YOUR LIVES?

"Forever busy with farm life and raising 5 children, we don't imagine our Mom put much direct thought into how she was, and still is, impacting our lives. Her actions just spoke for her. While canning Christmas pudding and rolling out Swedish thin bread, we learned that our heritage is not to be forgotten. When rolling ginger snap cookie dough in sugar, we learned that the secret ingredient to great baking is love. As much as we love fresh veggies from the garden, we know that no garden is complete without flowers to pick. From helping her serve dinner theatre meals to hundreds of people, we learned that though the stars are often seen as those on centre-stage, the show can't go on without those working hard behind the scenes. Like the Little Red Hen, we know that everything tastes better when you've grown the ingredients yourself, from beef to eggs to homemade jam. And it tastes better still when surrounded by family. She is the caregiver to our family tree. She planted our roots, nurtured us as we grew and should be proud of the way her branches have grown."

By the children of Marilyn Mitchell

FARMWIFE INTERVIEW #9
Name: Shirley Davidson

Age at this writing: 68

1. How long have you lived in this community?
   50 years. Moved to farm April 1965 when in-laws moved to town.

2. What was your background prior to marrying your husband?
   I went to school in Lloydminster. I lived in Vancouver for a year, took a business course and worked for Husky refinery in Lloyd in the office for 6 months before getting married.

3. How long have you been married, and if you have children - how many do you have?
   It was our 50-year anniversary in November, 2014. We have 4 children.

4. What has the role of the farmwife meant to you?
   Involved with doing cattle and seed and tax books. So, that kept me involved with what was going on in the farm.

5. What has your husbands' role been?
   The farming.

6. What is the best part, for you, in this life as a farmwife?
   Way of life.

7. What is the hardest part?
   Long hours during seeding and harvest.

8. Was feeling isolated ever a part of living on the farm? If so, how did you deal with it?
   No.

9. Were there any "new" traditions that you started in your family? (and may have passed down to your children)?
   Christmas Eve: the meal and the gift opening.

10. Was there anything you were not prepared for, prior to becoming a farmwife?

Fifty years ago, you just did what was expected of you and you never thought anything more about it.

11. Were there any expectations of you that proved especially difficult for you?
    I had chickens for a few yard, hated them.

12. Was there anything that you would have liked to (or that you did) change?
    More holiday time.

13. If there was a legacy that you'd like to leave behind from your life here, what would you like it to be? (Such as: your proudest accomplishment, or something important that you instilled in your children)?
    Enjoy life. Family is the most important thing.

14. What is your fallback recipe when you're too tired to plan for supper?
    Poached eggs on toast.

15. We've all had unexpected guests pop in. What was a trick that you used to ensure you were always prepared for company?
    Try and have some baking in freezer.

16. Do you have any words of advice for women who may be marrying a farmer today?
    Enjoy your life. Time goes by so fast.

17. What is a key piece of advice you could give to keep a marriage strong?
    Don't sweat the small stuff.

RECIPE FROM SHIRLEY DAVIDSON:
RIBS:

Simmer 2 racks of ribs for approximately 1-2 hours.

Sauce:

1 cup ketchup
½ cup honey
¼ cup soy sauce
6 cloves garlic (crushed)

Directions: drain ribs, put on sauce. Can be frozen at this time, or used. Put in oven, or on BBQ to heat.

RECIPE:

What is a favorite, signature recipe that you're willing to share?

Ribs
simmer 2 racks of ribs for approx 1-2 hrs.

Sauce   1 cup ketchup
         ½ cup honey
         ¼ cup soy sauce
         6 cloves garlic (crushed)

drain ribs – put on sauce. Can be frozen at
this time or used.
Put in oven or BBQ

Signed: SHIRLEY DAVIDSON

WHAT IS THE IMPACT YOUR MOTHER HAS HAD ON YOUR LIVES?

"I think the main things Mom has instilled in me are: the value of family, working hard, perseverance, and love. Sometimes growing up, I may have veered off course a couple of times, but by the example she leads her life by, I feel it always brought us back to what was right. She is a strong women who I admire, and whose example I base my daily life on.

It's because of her that I have the wonderful life I do have, and one that I'm grateful for. No matter where I am or where I live, when I go back to the farm there is no other place in the world I feel more at "home" and that is directly because of her. I feel that says a lot about how she raised her family. She is an amazing woman who I feel so lucky to call my Mom".

By, Lorelei Pugh, daughter of Shirley Davidson

FARMWIFE INTERVIEW #10
Name: Marilyn Wright

Age at this writing: 60

----

1. How long have you lived in this community?
   All my life. We live on the farm where I was raised.

2. What was your background prior to marrying your husband?
   I was raised on the farm. After high school grad, I worked in Lloyd at Evergreen Florists as a floral designer. We were married in October, right after harvest.

3. How long have you been married, and if you have children - how many do you have?
   40 years, October 27, 1973. 2 children … 5 grand children.

4. What has the role of the farmwife meant to you?
   A little bit of everything. All of the home and childcare. In the beginning, we lived in the Earlie District and had pigs and chickens that I did the majority of chores. Keith farmed with his Dad and brother. We didn't have enough land to live off so Keith had an oilfield job. I have always worked part-time and still am spare bus driver. After we moved to Rivercourse, we bought my family farm. Keith was able to farm full-time and so we worked on our own. That meant a more active role helping with cattle and field work. Mostly as the go-fer and truck driver, sprint and fall and also combining in fall. I have always been the farm book-keeper, so my role as farmwife has been as a partner.

5. What has your husbands' role been?
   Keith's role has been the "farmer" doing the majority of the farm work and decision making on crops and machinery and livestock. Although, we do discuss major purchases.

6. What is the best part, for you, in this life as a farmwife?
   Owning, managing, working together, and building our own "family" business and the freedom in the not so busy times to be able to take time to pursue other interests. Being able to keep the farm in the family.

7. What is the hardest part?

The stress. Worrying about the weather and marketing and commodity prices. All things we can't control but have a huge effect on us.

8. Was feeling isolated ever a part of living on the farm? If so, how did you deal with it?

No, feeling isolated has never been an issue. I grew up on the farm so being a few miles away from friends, neighbors and services has always been a way of life. It has never been a problem to hop in our car to go have coffee with a neighbor or borrow something to save a trip to town as we didn't always go as often as we do now. If we felt the need to talk with someone but couldn't get away we'd pick up the phone and call a family member or friend. With everything so busy nowadays, I enjoy having a quiet, solitary day at home!

9. Were there any "new" traditions that you started in your family? (and may have passed down to your children)?

No, I don't think I started any new traditions. As our family grows, life is constantly changing so we have tried to be flexible and just go with the flow, sometimes changing dates as needed. I have tried to keep holidays "special occasions" and include children/ grandchildren in planning events, decorating, baking, etc.

10. Was there anything you were not prepared for, prior to becoming a farmwife?

I was raised on the farm so I already knew most aspects. I don't think anyone expected input costs to raise so dramatically or that it (farming) would go from a simple way of life to a big business. We are just the 2nd generation farming so it has been a learning curve in going from "the kid" to parent/owner to sharing all that with our son and his wife and children with no previous generations to share advice and experiences of how to handle all the differing dynamics.

11. Were there any expectations of you that proved especially difficult for you?

Just having to know so many aspects of farming is always a challenge and being readily available when called to help no matter what you might be doing.

12. Was there anything that you would have liked to (or that you did) change?

The only thing I would and tried to change was the old traditional idea that the wife stay home to raise children, look after the home and be there to help with the farm. I have always gotten out to work part-time and do volunteering, but I would certainly appreciate more help with our home and yard.

13. If there was a legacy that you'd like to leave behind from your life here, what would you like it to be? (Such as: your proudest accomplishment, or something important that you instilled in your children)?

I've always tried to teach my children to get along with people and treat them how they would like to be treated. Do what you can to help your family and community.

14. What is your fallback recipe when you're too tired to plan for supper?
Spicy Hamburger Skillet

Brown 1 hamburger (drain grease off)
Add: 1 jar chunky salsa, 1 jar hot water, 2 c pasta (fusili or macaroni)
Simmer 10 minutes until pasta is cooked, grate cheese over top, let melt and serve with salad or fresh veggies.

15. We've all had unexpected guests pop in. What was a trick that you used to ensure you were always prepared for company?

In summer, BBQ. Winter - make a pot of soup, hamburger and veggies if time, or a quick corn and potato chowder and biscuits. Plus, I try to keep an apple pie in the freezer.

16. Do you have any words of advice for women who may be marrying a farmer today?

Patience, patience, patience! Be flexible, we are on call 24/7 and plans can change at the drop of a hat.

17. What is a key piece of advice you could give to keep a marriage strong?

Besides patience - communicate. Life is so much easier if we know what the other is thinking or doing.

RECIPE FROM MARILYN WRIGHT:
APPLE SAUCE CAKE:

Ingredients:

2 ½ cup flour
½ cup sugar
1 tsp baking soda
2 ½ tsp baking powder
½ tsp salt
½ tsp cinnamon
1 tsp vanilla
¼ cup oil
½ cup milk
1 egg
1 cup applesauce
1 cup chopped apple

Topping:

Boil for 1 minute: 1/3 cup margarine and ¾ cup brown sugar
Add: 3 tbsp cream or milk

Bring to a boil.

Sprinkle ¾ - 1 cup coconut over cake.

Spread sauce over and broil for 8 minutes.

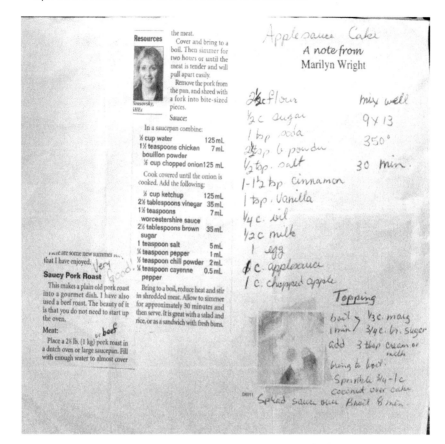

Resources

Grasovsky, SHEx

the meat.
Cover and bring to a boil. Then simmer for two hours or until the meat is tender and will pull apart easily.

Remove the pork from the pan, and shred with a fork into bite-sized pieces.

Sauce:

In a saucepan combine:

½ cup water	125 mL
1½ teaspoons chicken bouillon powder	7 mL
½ cup chopped onion	125 mL

Cook covered until the onion is cooked. Add the following:

½ cup ketchup	125 mL
2½ tablespoons vinegar	35 mL
1½ teaspoons worcestershire sauce	7 mL
2½ tablespoons brown sugar	35 mL
1 teaspoon salt	5 mL
¼ teaspoon pepper	1 mL
½ teaspoon chili powder	2 mL
¼ teaspoon cayenne pepper	0.5 mL

Bring to a boil, reduce heat and stir in shredded meat. Allow to simmer for approximately 30 minutes and then serve. It is great with a salad and rice, or as a sandwich with fresh buns.

...re are some new summer ... that I have enjoyed. *Very Good!*

Saucy Pork Roast

This makes a plain old pork roast into a gourmet dish. I have also used a beef roast. The beauty of it is that you do not need to start up the oven.

Meat: *or beef*

Place a 2½ lb. (1 kg) pork roast in a dutch oven or large saucepan. Fill with enough water to almost cover

Applesauce Cake

A note from
Marilyn Wright

2½ c flour
½ c sugar
1 tsp. soda
2 tsp. b. powder
½ tsp. salt
1 - 1½ tsp. cinnamon
1 tsp. vanilla
¼ c. oil
½ c milk
1 egg
¾ c. applesauce
1 c. chopped apple

mix well
9 x 13
350°
30 min.

Topping

boil > ⅓ c. marg
1 min > ¾ c. br. sugar
add 3 tbsp cream or milk
bring to boil.
Sprinkle ¾ - 1 c
coconut over cake
Spread sauce over Broil 8 min.

FARMWIFE INTERVIEW #11
Name: Glenda "Penny" Johansson

Age at this writing: 78

1. How long have you lived in this community?

    I lived in the Wildwood Community until marrying Carl at age 17.

2. What was your background prior to marrying your husband?

    I lived in the Wildwood community on my family farm and went to school there until grade 9. In grade 10 I went to Kitscoty. After that, I worked at the Treasury Branch in Lloydminster. I had 4 sisters and 1 brother. I was the 3rd in line. I met Carl at 16.

3. How long have you been married, and if you have children - how many do you have?

    We were married on March 31, 1954. We have 2 kids: Jackie and Glen.

4. What has the role of the farmwife meant to you?

    "I didn't do anything … I just lived here and did what others did before me". I just milked cows to sell the cream, baled straw, cooked, cleaned, hauled grain from the combine. Oh yeah, and we didn't have power in the beginning. Carl: "she was a slave".

5. What has your husbands' role been?

    All outdoor farm work and he was a good provider.

6. What is the best part, for you, in this life as a farmwife?

    Best part was raising kids on the farm, we had a very active community at that time, too.

7. What is the hardest part?

    The financial hardship was hard. When we were broke, we were "broke". One time we wanted to go to a movie in Paradise Valley, it would cost .35c each … we didn't have. We just laughed.

8. Was feeling isolated ever a part of living on the farm? If so, how did you deal with it?

When the roads were blocked, yes. But, when the roads allowed, there was always a lot of visiting, so I didn't feel lonely.

9. Were there any "new" traditions that you started in your family? (and may have passed down to your children)?

Christmas was and is still a tradition. We have a tree and turkey every year.

10. Was there anything you were not prepared for, prior to becoming a farmwife?

I didn't think much of it … because I didn't know any different.

11. Were there any expectations of you that proved especially difficult for you?

I always helped at home but didn't have a "full" idea of all that my Mom did.

12. Was there anything that you would have liked to (or that you did) change?

If there was anything I was unsure of how to do, I learned a lot from my Mother in law.

13. If there was a legacy that you'd like to leave behind from your life here, what would you like it to be? (Such as: your proudest accomplishment, or something important that you instilled in your children)?

The Johansson family was respected … I'd like to be seen as the same. I tried to teach my children honesty and fairness through my actions.

14. What is your fallback recipe when you're too tired to plan for supper?

Macaroni with tomatoes and cheese.

15. We've all had unexpected guests pop in. What was a trick that you used to ensure you were always prepared for company?

I didn't have a trick - we always had something. Carl (husband): "my mom was funny … … on Sundays around 10am, somebody was always coming by to visit. She would run out back and catch two chickens and pluck them so we could have fried chicken".

16. Do you have any words of advice for women who may be marrying a farmer today?
    Enjoy it! It's quiet. It's a good place to raise children. They learn a lot.

17. What is a key piece of advice you could give to keep a marriage strong?
    Respect one another.

RECIPE FROM PENNY JOHANSSON:
BUTTER TARTS:

Melt 1/3 cup butter and ¾ cup brown sugar and then, let cool.

Beat into it: 2 eggs, 2 tbsp milk, and 1 tsp vanilla.

If you'd like, add raisins, or currants.

Bake for 20 minutes at 350F.

Butter Tarts

1/3 cup butter   } melt and
3/4 cup brown sugar } let cool
        Beat into it

2 eggs
2 tablespoons milk
1 teaspoon vanilla

If you like add raisins currants or
Bake 20 min at 350° F.   nuts

FARMWIFE INTERVIEW #12
Name: Lois Purser

Lois Purser stands with her daughter, Dana on a Mom/Daughter trip to Atlantic Canada in the Fall of 2015. Age at this writing: 56

Farmwives in Profile

1. How long have you lived in this community?

    I have lived in the Vanesti school district near Paradise Valley since I was married in 1978. Before that, I grew up just south of McLaughlin … so 36 years.

2. What was your background prior to marrying your husband?

    I was a farm girl. I went to the city for college after high school but missed my high school sweetheart and moved back home, worked in Lloydminster and soon after was engaged.

3. How long have you been married, and if you have children - how many do you have?

    36 years. We have 2 children (we say we have 3, as our first child was stillborn at full term and she is in our hearts always).

4. What has the role of the farmwife meant to you?

    We have farmed with my husband's father in partnership. In later years, he has taken a backseat and we have a more major role. Although I have never had to be in on the daily chores much, I enjoyed helping with the cattle and combining once the kids were older. Mostly yard work, gardening and sharing meals with my mother-in-law while she was alive.

5. What has your husbands' role been?

    From partnering decisions to now total control, with advice and support from his Dad. He also does all the books!

6. What is the best part, for you, in this life as a farmwife?

    Freedom to raise your children in a clean, wholesome, healthy environment. They can learn a good work ethic. If you need to scream - do it! ha! We have lived in the same yard as my inlaws (it was the 'best' situation to raise our children and now our son and family are here in the yard along with Great Grandpa - 4 generations! I had an awesome Mother-in-law and have a wonderful father-in-law and daughter in-law, I am so lucky, I know!

7. What is the hardest part?

Remote location from cities and entertainment (neighbors become precious). Being adaptable - plans change in minutes. Working around others plans, due to weather or unexpected chores.

8. Were there ever times that you felt isolated as a farmwife, or because of living on a farm?

Over the years I have had times when I wished we lived closer to town or the city but I'm happy we don't. I 've always had access to a vehicle so was lucky. As soon as the roads are blocked with a storm, I'd like out!!, think that is everyone.

I often think of my Mom, how she must have felt, not having a drivers license. Long hours alone without any way of reaching Dad, we are so lucky! Times change, i cant imagine not having the freedom go anywhere anytime! Although it's nice to just stay home without commitment also.

9. Were there any "new" traditions that you started in your family? (and may have passed down to your children)?

July 1 at home or at the cabin - we always have a BBQ turkey. One of our kids birthdays is in harvest, so lots of years - birthday cake in the field - was fun! Cover silage pit (whole family).

10. Was there anything you were not prepared for, prior to becoming a farmwife?

Being raised on a farm, I thought I knew everything, but was very young, naive, and probably selfish. My Mom was a phone call away for advice. Ha!

11. Were there any expectations of you that proved especially difficult for you?

It took me years to accept not being in control of organizing everyone's life - can't be done!

12. Was there anything that you would have liked to (or that you did) change?

    The more I think about it (nothing significant).

13. If there was a legacy that you'd like to leave behind from your life here, what would you like it to be? (Such as: your proudest accomplishment, or something important that you instilled in your children)?

    How important family is/to be cherished. My kids are my greatest accomplishment. They are strong, kind people - who could ask for more! Our kids were expected to get an education away from the farm even if they were going to come back to the farm.

14. What is your fallback recipe when you're too tired to plan for supper?
Omelets

    Pancakes
    Hotdogs
    Sad, but true!

15. We've all had unexpected guests pop in. What was a trick that you used to ensure you were always prepared for company?

    Try to keep front room tidy and have company always come through the front door!

16. Do you have any words of advice for women who may be marrying a farmer today?

    Be prepared to be alone in busy seasons and not have help from Daddy. (Things to have changed some in this area since we had little ones - don't know how they do it! ha!) Learn how to do the 'honey do list' jobs on your own, or be patient!

17. What is a key piece of advice you could give to keep a marriage strong?

Be adaptable and supportive - plans can change quickly - go with the flow. (I think this got easier with age)! Keep communication open.

RECIPE FROM LOIS PURSER:
YORKSHIRE PUDDINGS:

Ingredients:

1 cup flour
¼ tsp salt
¾ cup milk
¼ cup water
4 eggs

Directions: Combine mild and water. Whisk in flour and salt. Add eggs, one by one, beating after each. Grease and flour muffin tins. Fill with batter ¾ full. Bake at 450F for 10-15 minutes.

Enjoy with roast beef dinner!

RECIPE:

What is a favorite, signature recipe that you're willing to share?

Yorkshire Puddings

1 c. flour
1/4 teas. salt
3/4 c. milk
1/4 c. water
4 eggs

Combine milk + water. Whisk
in flour + salt. Add eggs one
by one beating after each.
Grease + flour muffin tins
Fill with batter 3/4 full
Bake 450 – 10-15 min

Enjoy w/ roast beef dinner.

Signed: *Lois Purser*

WHAT IS THE IMPACT YOUR MOTHER HAS HAD ON YOUR LIVES?

"My Mother would have liked to see me marry a lawyer or a doctor. Instead, I am now living on a farm with a Mechanic/ Farmer. I know she understands why I want to live a life which I have grown up with, and which has instilled such deep values in me. However, she also knows firsthand that it is a hard life. A life where money doesn't come easy, work is hard, and there are sacrifices to be made. A life where I have seen my parents unselfishly provide everything they could for my brother and I.

I feel that my mother has lived her life in a way that she can be there to always support us through our struggles and successes. Even now, she is only a phone call away and shows a dependable and caring support in all that I do. I honestly do not remember my Mother ever missing a hockey game, sports event, music recital, rehearsal, and the list goes on. Even during busy times of year on the farm there would be coffee and treats in the field and big meals on the table. Every birthday/holiday was celebrated with a big cake and meal, often a party, and surrounded by friends and family. She has also taught me the importance of family by making sure that we keep in contact with relatives often and support one another. She knows the importance of hard work but also the importance of balance in life and taking a deserved break. Although we didn't grow up in a big city, my parents made sure that we still had opportunities to go see musicals, concerts, hockey games, and do some traveling including Mexico and Disneyland. My Mother is also extremely organized and these skills have luckily been passed on to my Brother and I who are famous for making lists, having dates on the calendar, and arriving early for events. The importance of volunteering and being present in a small community was also something our family modeled to us in words, and in their actions.

If I do end up becoming a farmwife/mother myself one day, my mother has definitely been a very big inspiration, and I hope that I can pull it off with as near as much class as she has."

By, the children of Lois Purser

FARMWIFE INTERVIEW #13
Name: Charleen Teasdale

Age at this writing: 61

long have you lived in this community?
years.

2. What was your background prior to marrying your husband?
I was a teacher, as a child I lived on a farm where my Dad was a hired hand. There was, and maybe there will is a stigma attached to being a hired man.

3. How long have you been married, and if you have children - how many do you have?
We have been married 36 years and have 3 children.

4. What has the role of farmwife meant to you?
Offering support, emotionally and physically, and being a listener. Creating a nurturing environment for my husband and my kids.

5. What has your husbands' role been?
The rock and anchor, having the whole picture: plan and economics in his head and heart. My teammate in raising our family.

6. What is the best part, for you, in this life as a farmwife?
Having family, my husband, kids, parents and in-laws around, almost 24/7. Being connected.

7. What is the hardest part?
Having so many things out of our control no matter how hard we worked. Ie. weather, prices, BSE[2].

---

2   Bovine spongiform encephalopathy (BSE), commonly known as mad cow disease, is a fatal neurodegenerative disease (encephalopathy) in cattle that causes a spongy degeneration in the brain and spinal cord. BSE hit the area (and beef prices) hard in 2003.

8. Was feeling isolated ever a part of living on the farm? If so, how did you deal with it?

At times there was a feeling of aloneness, not exactly isolation. Being shy by nature, I guess I coped best by sticking my nose in a book.

9. Were there any "new" traditions that you started in your family? (and may have passed down to your children)?

Being an elementary teacher I think I have brought a child-like excitement to holidays. It was met with many a raised eyebrow from my mother-in-law; but we continue to do silly and special things and I see my kids including a lot of them in their families.

10. Was there anything you were not prepared for, prior to becoming a farmwife?

The long hours alone with the kids when they were babies, during harvest.

11. Were there any expectations of you that proved especially difficult for you?

I'm not very mechanical and don't have a lot of confidence, even now, in running the equipment, but I do it when called upon. I never volunteer ;)

12. Was there anything that you would have liked to (or that you did) change?

Having more confidence to jump in and handle equipment, it would have made things easier for my husband, however, our kids needed me too. I always was there for their school and sports.

13. If there was a legacy that you'd like to leave behind from your life here, what would you like it to be? (Such as: your proudest accomplishment, or something important that you instilled in your children)?

That the children whose lives I have touched, my three, our god-daughters, our grandchildren, my students, the neighbor kids, knew that I truly cared. That I be remembered as a kind and thoughtful human being.

14. What is your fallback recipe when you're too tired to plan for supper?
Pancakes and bacon or sausages.

15. We've all had unexpected guests pop in. What was a trick that you used to ensure you were always prepared for company?
Having a container of cookies or muffins in the freezer, but in these later years, a package of Golden Oreos works great too. Who really cares?

16. Do you have any words of advice for women who may be marrying a farmer today?
Listen to him, be supportive every way you can, this isn't just his job, it's his life and ultimately yours too.

17. What is a key piece of advice you could give to keep a marriage strong?
Communication.

RECIPE FROM CHARLEEN TEASDALE:
JIM'S 2X2 PANCAKES:

Ingredients:

2 cups of flour
2 tbsp white sugar
2 tsp baking powder
pinch of salt

2 eggs

2 tbsp canola oil
2 cups milk

Directions:

Stir together, only until well blended. Pour into hot griddle or fry pan which has been slightly oiled. When bubbles appear, flip and cook briefly.

Enjoy with butter and Rogers Golden Syrup

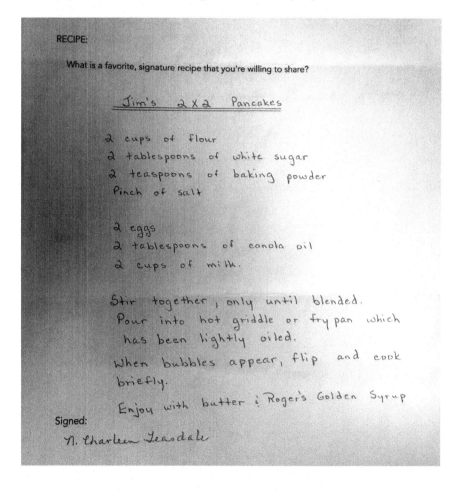

RECIPE:

What is a favorite, signature recipe that you're willing to share?

Jim's 2 X 2 Pancakes

2 cups of flour
2 tablespoons of white sugar
2 teaspoons of baking powder
Pinch of salt

2 eggs
2 tablespoons of canola oil
2 cups of milk.

Stir together, only until blended.
Pour into hot griddle or fry pan which has been lightly oiled.
When bubbles appear, flip and cook briefly.

Enjoy with butter & Roger's Golden Syrup

Signed:
N. Charleen Teasdale

WHAT IS THE IMPACT YOUR MOTHER HAS HAD ON YOUR LIVES?

"No matter what the event, the situation or the issue, our mother was never far away. To this day she is selfless and drops everything to help her children and grandchildren. To be a farmwife you are required to have more than one occupation: taxi driver, chef, caregiver, bookkeeper, teacher, veterinary assistant, carpenter, nurse, etc. Mom was always willing to take on these roles, even if it required more than one at a time. We have always been able to count on her for support and encouragement.

Growing up, we were privileged to have packed lunches with farm veggies, homemade cookies and snacks. After school we could always count on smelling fresh baking and warm hot chocolate when we got off the bus. She always timed it perfectly! No matter what sport or extracurricular activity we tried, she was always cheering us on in the stands.

It's hard to remember a time when we would find her resting or sitting down. She always said that if Dad was working, so should she. There has never been a project too large for her to take on. She takes on all tasks willingly and is eager to learn something new. With her there is no job discrimination. If Dad was busy working in the field she was always determined to get the job done herself. She was never afraid to dig for tools and supplies in the shop.

To this day, she continues to demonstrate the hard work, selflessness, and self-reliance that we can only hope have rubbed off on us, and will continue through to the next generation."

By, the children of Charleen Teasdale

FARMWIFE INTERVIEW #14
Name: Shirley Deaville

Age at this writing: 67 years

1. How long have you lived in this community?
   Since 1969 - 44 years.

2. What was your background prior to marrying your husband?
   I was born and raised on a farm north of Edgerton, finished grade 12 there and took Medical Lab Tech at NAIT and U of A Hospital and worked there 2 years.

3. How long have you been married, and if you have children - how many do you have?
   Since July 1968 (45 years), we have 4 daughters.

4. What has the role of farmwife meant to you?
   Being a support by helping with decisions and working on the farm - yard and house work and some truck driving - hauling grain in spring and fall and helping where needed along with raising the family.

5. What has your husbands' role been?
Managing and running the farm in all aspects.

6. What is the best part, for you, in this life as a farmwife?
   I enjoy being on the farm and helping with the work and decisions. I was happy to be able to reuse the children on the farm.

7. What is the hardest part?
   I suppose dealing with the weather - hail, winds, tornadoes, a major drought year, and the extreme cold and snowy winters.

8. Was feeling isolated ever a part of living on the farm? If so, how did you deal with it?
   Possibly it was when the kids were young and you weren't as involved in other groups, etc. It surprised me when I felt it because I was from the farm. The isolation wasn't there for long though. It's not that I didn't know people, but it was harder to get out and do things.

9. Were there any "new" traditions that you started in your family? (and may have passed down to your children)?

With regards to food at family get togethers - as son in laws and other members joined - some nationality dishes - cabbage rolls, perogies - special desserts enjoyed.

10. Was there anything you were not prepared for, prior to becoming a farmwife?

The money spent on a farm just to maintain machinery and cropping costs. It has increased so much each year.

11. Were there any expectations of you that proved especially difficult for you?

Maybe at the time, but none that I remember now.

12. Was there anything that you would have liked to (or that you did) change?

(left blank)

13. If there was a legacy that you'd like to leave behind from your life here, what would you like it to be? (Such as: your proudest accomplishment, or something important that you instilled in your children)?

Work hard - never hurts anyone. Set goals for accomplishments and rewards.

14. What is your fallback recipe when you're too tired to plan for supper?

Bacon, eggs and pancakes
Grilled cheese sandwiches
Creamed salmon on toast.

15. We've all had unexpected guests pop in. What was a trick that you used to ensure you were always prepared for company?

Have food baked in freezer or frozen homemade soups, lasagnas.

16. Do you have any words of advice for women who may be marrying a farmer today?

Enjoy the lifestyle and be willing to be involved and helpful. Save a day or two for yourself and the ladies to enjoy some time.

17. What is a key piece of advice you could give to keep a marriage strong?

I don't know the real secret for that. Push for your marriage … make time. Communicate what is important to you.

RECIPE FROM SHIRLEY DEAVILLE:
JELLY ROLL:

Step 1: Beat 4 egg whites until soft peaks. Gradually add 125 ml of sugar and beat until stiff peaks.

Step 2: Beat 4 egg yolks until thick and lemon colored. Gradually add 60 ml sugar and 2 ml vanilla.

Step 3: Fold yolks carefully into whites.

Step 4: Stir in 175 ml flour, 2 ml salt, 5 ml baking powder. Line in a greased jelly roll pan with wax paper and grease again. Dust with flour. Pour mixture evenly and bake at 370F for 12-15 minutes. Sprinkle icing sugar on a clean tea towel and flip jelly roll on towel. Take off wax paper. Roll up jelly roll. Cool. Later full with lemon filling for jelly.

Jelly Roll

Step 1. Beat 4 egg whites until soft peaks. Gradually add 125 ml sugar + beat until stiff peaks.

Step 2. Beat 4 egg yolks until thick lemon colored. Gradually add 60 ml sugar + 2ml vanilla

Step 3. Fold yolks carefully into whites

Step 4. Stir in 175ml flour, 2ml salt, 5ml baking powder

Line a greased jelly roll pan with wax paper + grease again. Dust with flour. Pour mixture evenly + bake 370° for 12-15 min. Sprinkle icing sugar on a clean tea towel and flip jelly roll on towel. Take off wax paper. Roll up jelly roll. Cool. Later fill with lemon filling or jelly.

Shirley Deville

WHAT IS THE IMPACT YOUR MOTHER HAS HAD ON YOUR LIVES?

"The effect mom has had on our lives comes from the values she instilled in us while growing up on the farm. She showed the value of hard work every day with her "lets get something done" attitude, whether it be helping with the farm, working in the garden or making meals. She always encouraged us to "pitch in and help out" both at home and in community events.

Mom kept everything going by being well organized. She was always prepared and liked arriving somewhere early (a value we are still trying to perfect ourselves!)

Preparing large meals does not seem to trouble her. When company would just "pop in", delicious dinners and desserts seemed to magically appear! The effect of this on us has been to "double-batch" every baking recipe...just in case.

Although Mom's hands were always busy, her heart and ears were always open. She values education and encouraged us to follow our interests and studies, as she is interested in learning herself.

She is a great Mom, and we all look up to her."

By, the children of Shirley Deaville

FARMWIFE INTERVIEW #15
Name: Gladys Quinn

Age at this writing: 85

1. How long have you lived in this community?
   I have lived here 65 years.

2. What was your background prior to marrying your husband?
   I came from McLaughlin, AB. I came from a farming family with 10 kids in total. There were 5 boys and 5 girls in my family.

3. How long have you been married, and if you have children - how many do you have?
   I married Bill Quinn on May 25, 1949 and we had 4 children.

4. What has the role of farmwife meant to you?
   I had a milk cow, took care of chickens, turkeys, some work with pigs, took care of the "inside" work and took care of our kids.

5. What has your husbands' role been?
   Bill looked after the outside work in the fields with our 3 boys and a farmhand.

6. What is the best part, for you, in this life as a farmwife?
   Looking after the kids and gardening.

7. What is the hardest part?
   Keeping kids clean, they were always dirty! I hated working with the pigs … I was scared of them.

8. Was feeling isolated ever a part of living on the farm? If so, how did you deal with it?
   I didn't ever feel lonely at all. Bill's folks lived close to us and we saw them every day. It was just like home. After Bill passed away, loneliness set in, however. Now, it never goes away...

9. Were there any "new" traditions that you started in your family? (and may have passed down to your children)?
   Although, this wasn't a "new" tradition, but one I kept going in our family was we always celebrated Christmas on Christmas

Eve. We went to our Moms, then when there were too many people to fit there, we came to our house.

10. Was there anything you were not prepared for, prior to becoming a farmwife?

I would say doing some of the outside work with Bill, such as driving the tractor.

11. Were there any expectations of you that proved especially difficult for you?

Well, sometimes I had to learn these things (like driving an old tractor we had) without much instruction, so there were some close calls.

12. Was there anything that you would have liked to (or that you did) change?

Certain things in our old house … for example, while the kids were young, we had 3 bedrooms and they always complained about sharing rooms.

13. If there was a legacy that you'd like to leave behind from your life here, what would you like it to be? (Such as: your proudest accomplishment, or something important that you instilled in your children)?

I always canned, sewed and gardened. I was very often known for sewing skills … I used to make bridesmaid dresses.

14. What is your fallback recipe when you're too tired to plan for supper?

Pancakes.

15. We've all had unexpected guests pop in. What was a trick that you used to ensure you were always prepared for company?

I always had baking around. Donuts, especially.

16. Do you have any words of advice for women who may be marrying a farmer today?

Be open to going out to work with your husband from time to time.

17. What is a key piece of advice you could give to keep a marriage strong?

Do as many things together as you can.

RECIPE FROM GLADYS QUINN:

Spanish Macaroni:

2 cups macaroni cooked until tender
2 slices of chopped up bacon
1 large onion chopped up
3 large sticks of celery chopped in ½ inch pieces
¾ lb hamburger
½ lb cheddar cheese cut up into pieces
1 tin of tomato soup
1 can of sliced mushrooms
Salt and pepper to taste

Directions:

Brown bacon, onion, and celery in large pan.
Add hamburger and brown until well done.

In large bowl: put in macaroni, cheese,
soup, mushrooms and seasoning.

Add the meat mixture and mix well. If too
thick, add liquid from mushrooms.

Bake in greased casserole dish for 1 hour at 350F.

RECIPE:

What is a favorite, signature recipe that you're willing to share?

Spanish Macaroni's

2 cups macaroni cooked till tender
2 slices of chopped up bacon
1 large onions chopped up
3 large sticks of celery chopped in small pieces
3/4 lb. of hamburger

Signed:

1/2 lb. cheddar cheese cut up in pieces
1 tin of tomato soup
1 tin of sliced mushrooms
Salt & Pepper to taste

Brown bacon, onion, celery in large pan
add hamburger and brown till well done
In large bowl put in macaroni, cheese
soup + mushrooms + seasoning. Add the
meat mixture and mix well. If too thick
add liquid from mushrooms.
Bake in greased casserole for 1 hour at 350°

Gladys Quinn

FARMWIFE INTERVIEW #16
Name: Dorothy Cooper

Dorothy Cooper stands with her husband Glen in front of their "proud red" equipment shortly before retiring from farming in 2014. Age at this writing: 60

Farmwives in Profile

1. How long have you lived in this community?
   I have lived here since April 1975.

2. What was your background prior to marrying your husband?
   Grew up on a farm west of Paradise Valley. Went from high school to Reeve's Business College, Lloydminster. Worked for Swift Insurance Adjusters.

3. How long have you been married, and if you have children - how many do you have?
   Been married for 39 years. We have 4 daughters.

4. What has the role of farmwife meant to you?
   It has meant that I have had to be very flexible in what I plan to do. The farm work had to come first and my role was to be there to help out.

5. What has your husbands' role been?
   My husbands' role has been to make the decisions that have to be made. Plan the work and do the work, without hired help.

6. What is the best part, for you, in this life as a farmwife?
   The best part is that you are living your life, with your family, while doing the job that you are making a living at. Some of the work becomes a way of life for the family.

7. What is the hardest part?
   The hardest part was when the kids were younger and into extra activities that interfered with farming, because those were very important as well.

8. Was feeling isolated ever a part of living on the farm? If so, how did you deal with it?
   I never did feel isolated or away from anything. I grew up on a farm in the country and at that time any big centre seemed far away. When I grew up and lived on the farm, we were always close enough to anything we needed or wanted. Our kids

thought we were a long way from anything when they were teenagers but it didn't ever stop them from going places. I loved the quietness and freedom of being in the country and never did feel isolated.

9. Were there any "new" traditions that you started in your family? (and may have passed down to your children)?

Most of the traditions, especially on the holidays (Christmas, Easter) were passed down from our families. I didn't really start new ones.

10. Was there anything you were not prepared for, prior to becoming a farmwife?

I probably didn't expect to be helping with the work on the farm as much as I did. We decided early that we weren't going to get so big we needed hired help to get the work done. So I then realized I had to help out.

11. Were there any expectations of you that proved especially difficult for you?

I was raised on a farm and helped with the farm work. So, I had some experience, which I was grateful for or I would have found it very difficult.

12. Was there anything that you would have liked to (or that you did) change?

We changed from harvesting with other family to strictly doing it on our own.

13. If there was a legacy that you'd like to leave behind from your life here, what would you like it to be? (Such as: your proudest accomplishment, or something important that you instilled in your children)?

That above all, family is important. That's why farm life went hand in hand with that. But, I know my children will not raise their kids on a farm. Even so, no matter what they do in their lives, family is the most important thing they will do.

14. What is your fallback recipe when you're too tired to plan for supper?

Pancakes and sausages.

15. We've all had unexpected guests pop in. What was a trick that you used to ensure you were always prepared for company?

The best way was to have a casserole and a pie in the freezer. Wasn't always there though! So, I wasn't always prepared.

16. Do you have any words of advice for women who may be marrying a farmer today?

Maybe farming has changed from when we started. But, I always thought your own career has to go on a back burner and your career has to change to concentrate on the farm. It takes both people as a couple to successfully do it.

17. What is a key piece of advice you could give to keep a marriage strong?

One fact is: Life does NOT carry on and you live "happily ever after". I'm not sure what advice I have, but some would be 1) to share the same future goals for yourselves and work towards them together. 2) Keep communication open and alive at all times. This means discussing things and really listening to what each other says. 3)Keep your own individual interests going, even if they are not mutual. But don't let them overtake your time. 4) Realize that there are going to be times that are hard and it will take a lot of work to get through them. 5) Keep a sense of humor in general.

RECIPE FROM DOROTHY COOPER:
HAMBURGER SOUP:

Step one:

1 lb hamburger
1 chopped onion
pinch garlic salt
Brown these all together.

Step 2:

Add the following and simmer:

1 large can diced tomatoes (or 1 quart home-canned)
2 medium diced potatoes
2 stalks celery
2 carrots diced
Any small amount of vegetables leftover in fridge
3 cups water
3 OXO boullion cubes (or similar)
Salt, pepper and parsley.

(If I don't put in potatoes, I put some macaroni in the last 10 minutes).

RECIPE:

What is a favorite, signature recipe that you're willing to share?

Hamburger Soup

1 lb. hamburger
1 chopped onion   Brown all
pinch garlic salt   together

Add following and simmer:

1 lg can diced tomatoes
2 med. diced potatoes (1 qt. home canned)
2 stalks celery
2 carrots diced
Any small amount of vegetables leftover in fridge.
3 cups water
3 oxo boullion cubes (or similar)
salt, pepper, parsley. ~~Simmer~~ Simmer ½ hr.
(If I don't put in potatoes. I put in some
macaroni the last 10 min.)

Signed: *Dorothy Cooper*

WHAT IS THE IMPACT YOUR MOTHER HAS HAD ON YOUR LIVES?

"The effect Mom had on our lives shows in many ways. Mom was the one that kept everything running, whether it was one of us, Dad, or her fulltime farm laborer and bookkeeping job. Aside from these full time jobs, she was also part time nurse, chef, vet, gardener, housekeeper, Executive assistant, coach … She made sure everyone was fed well, chauffeured one or four of us to dance, ringette, piano, brownies, ball, 4-H, friends; it was endless. She kept the house in order, constantly doing chores inside and out. She was the assistant mechanic, truck driver, feed lot laborer and quite often with one or more 'helpers' tagging along. She does not see these things as extraordinary, because 'that is just what you do'. These are also the many things that we kids have taken for granted over the years but can appreciate it so much more now that we have our own families (and we don't even have a farm to run). She has taught us hard work, selflessness and to try and appreciate the small things."

By, the children of Dorothy Cooper

FARMWIFE INTERVIEW #17
Name: Maureen Anderson

Maureen Anderson sits in the living room of her home she shares with her husband Stan. They moved off the farm in 2014 and now live in town. Age at this writing: 82

1. How long have you lived in this community?

   52 years (1941-1951 = 10 years and then from 1972-2013 - 41 years) Total= 52 years

2. What was your background prior to marrying your husband?

   Office - Accounts payables and receivables - telephones.

3. How long have you been married, and if you have children - how many do you have?

   44 years. Stan has 2 girls, and has also supported another girl which is not his - Maureen has 3 children, 1 boy and 2 girls and has lost one Patty Lee. Total 5 children.

4. What has the role of the farmwife meant to you?

   Everything - the love of all animals, especially horses. Loved working the land, seeing the newborn animals, calves, colts, pigs and loved raising chickens. Big garden. Lastly, enjoying the farm women in this district - exchanging recipes, attending home economic classes and outings.

5. What has your husbands' role been?

   Farming (mixed), oilfield consultant, willing community worker, kitscoty golf course member, director and maintenance, vice president of legion, sergeant at arms member of crime watch, maintenance at kitscoty seniors, volunteer for blood service for the city of lloydminster.

6. What is the best part, for you, in this life as a farmwife?

   Being my own boss. Freedom to do the many things I always wanted to do and having the time to create new ventures in life. Allowing me to work for Stats Canada and various clubs I belonged to re. Court Lady K, PV Legion, Coordinate Blood Services for the City of Lloydminster, Canvasor for the Heart and Stroke, bowling, caring for my Mom and Mary ???, Lots of babysitting grandchildren.

7. What is the hardest part?

Operating the farm when Stan was away consulting and away from home.

8. Was feeling isolated ever a part of living on the farm? If so, how did you deal with it?

Never in my life.

9. Were there any "new" traditions that you started in your family? (and may have passed down to your children)?

No hats or caps allowed to be worn at the meal table. The 3 things I instilled in my children - do not steal, cheat or lie - this was always told to my sister and myself by my Father James A O'Neill.

10. Was there anything you were not prepared for, prior to becoming a farmwife?

Because I had lived as a child on the farm and had worked the land with my father with horses; I had to learn how to drive a tractor, combine, grain truck, calve out cows - these were a few of the things I was not prepared for - however Stan taught me and I loved every moment of it.

11. Were there any expectations of you that proved especially difficult for you?

No.

12. Was there anything that you would have liked to (or that you did) change?

Change the condition of the water, I would have liked to have had more time with my horses, and of course more of them.

13. If there was a legacy that you'd like to leave behind from your life here - (for example, something important to you that would be instilled in your children; or one of your proudest accomplishments) - what would you like it to be?

Giving of themselves to help other people, take time to share and care for loved ones, volunteer to help others, donate blood of you can, be available to help less fortunate, be thrifty with your hard earned money, take care of your clothes, to always be presentable, don't be afraid to ask God for help in time of need and be humble.

14. What is your fallback recipe when you're too tired to plan for supper?

Having homemade soup from the deep freeze with toasted homemade buns/bread and fruit.

15. We've all had unexpected guests pop in. What was a trick that you used to ensure you were always prepared for company?

Previously prepared stew, goulash, buns and pie from the deepfreeze.

16. Do you have any words of advice for women who may be marrying a farmer today?

It is the best life in the world, a great place to raise a family. Become involved in your community, work together and play together.

17. What is a key piece of advice you could give to keep a marriage strong?

Every day that you get up, give each other a hug. Something I promised Stan a long time ago is: at breakfast, I will have my hair combed and done if you shave. And, we both have.

RECIPE(S) FROM MAUREEN ANDERSON:
CHICKEN AND RICE:

Preheat oven to 350-375F.

1 cup uncooked rice. Sprinkle on bottom of a large baking pan (13X9 inch or similar).

1 cut up fryer chicken (or chicken breasts, cut up). Arrange on top of rice.

1 package dry onion soup - sprinkle over chicken evenly. (I use ½ packet).

1 can celery soup, diluted as directed on can. (Usually 1 can of water). Cover the pan tightly with foil. Bake for 1 ½ - 2 hours. This can be thrown together quickly, and doesn't have to be watched. We like it very much and find it's a good "lazy woman" recipe.

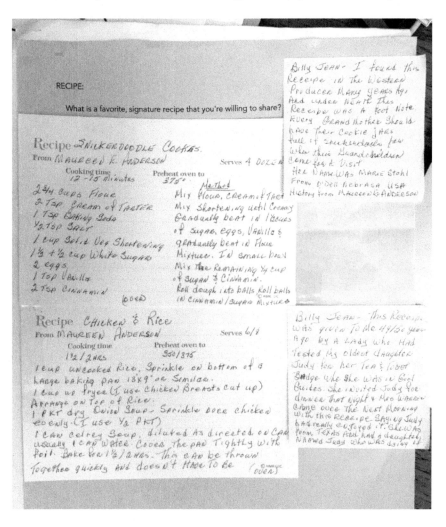

SNICKERDOODLE COOKIES:

2 2/3 cups flour
2 tsp cream of tarter
1 tsp baking soda
½ tsp salt
1 cup solid vegetables shortening
1 ½ plus ½ cup white sugar
2 eggs
1 tsp vanilla
2 tsp cinnamon

Method:

Mix flour, cream of tarter. Mix shortening until creamy. Gradually beat in 1 ½ cups sugar, eggs, vanilla and gradually beat in the flour mixture.

In small bowl, mix the remaining ¼ cup sugar and cinnamon.

Roll dough into balls, roll balls in cinnamon/ sugar mixture. Place on ungreased baking sheets about 2 inches apart. Cool and enjoy!

** AUTHOR'S NOTE ABOUT RECIPES:

Recipes have been transcribed verbatim and have not been tested. Photo of recipe is following each transcription. Always err on side of image.

CONCLUSION:

Since I asked these women some very personal questions, it's only fair I share too. There are a lot of reasons I wanted to do this book, but I know now that the primary reason I was drawn to bringing this idea to fruition was to help me to completely feel the peace of this place I now call home. Not all of us come from such stability, grounding and strength so my appreciation for being witness to it is deep and genuine.

The gratitude I have for these seventeen women sharing their hearts with me is indescribable. From the candid conversations as we had as we shared tea, canned peaches, or shared tears about the loneliness since the loss of their true love - I appreciated every word. The overarching theme of my interviews is that few of these women complained. They were grateful for their ability to raise their children in a farm environment, and they bonded together as women and as community members. This has been beyond inspiring to me.

The concept of "home" has never been a "static" concept in my life up until now. It has been a moving, changing entity that I struggled and longed to find. I have now found it, and I can't imagine it being in a more idyllic place.

I have learned so many lessons throughout the creation of this book. I've learned how lucky I am to have received "marriage advice" from a combined 600+ years of married life. Not many people can say they've had so much wisdom shared with them. I am so grateful for this.

I have learned other amazing nuggets, as well, reminding me to listen to my own heart about what is right for me and my family. I have learned that I am surrounded by amazing tradition and we can take the good of that on into our futures, and make the "changes" that are right for us.

As some of the women told me: they felt they had 3 options – a secretary, a nurse, or a teacher (that was if you could afford to go to school). To those that put all of your time, heart and soul into the caring for your homes and families - you are treasures.

As one women told me after her interview, though, that "it's only good for the kids if it's good for the Mom" to be a full-time stay at home parent. So, to those that feel their "fullest" and most "at peace" to work out of the home – do not doubt yourself, you are doing right by your children.

It is not a competition: to all of us and however we choose to walk this life - may we feel loved, respected, and "full" in our soul. I have been blessed to have landed in this place, and to carve out a "purpose" that is perfect for me. I have the family and life that I truly love now - and although the roles of a "farmwife" may be changing - I will be forever grateful for the lessons learned interviewing these women. I love this community, and so to the people here: thank you for welcoming me.

"These women have been the pillars holding these communities up for a very long time and must be celebrated."

– Billi J Miller

ABOUT THE AUTHOR

Previously on a career path in Government in the city, Billi J Miller happily gave it up to marry the "Farmer" of her dreams and live in the country in 2010. She has since created 2 successful photography businesses where she photographs farm families "while at work", and creates and sells fine art photography.

Her award-winning work has been recognized and on display at numerous venues. She is a member of the Professional Writers Association of Canada (PWAC) and she freelance writes for newsprint + magazines.

She resides with her husband and their 2 young girls on a 100-year old farm in Alberta, Canada.

You can find her work here: www.billijmillerphotography.com.

CPSIA information can be obtained
at www.ICGtesting.com
Printed in the USA
LVOW01s1214280116

472585LV00025B/216/P